Shakespeare and Eastern Europe

Oxford Shakespeare Topics

GENERAL EDITORS: PETER HOLLAND AND STANLEY WELLS

Shakespeare and Eastern Europe

ZDENĚK STŘÍBRNÝ

OXFORD
UNIVERSITY PRESS

Great Clarendon Street, Oxford OX2 6DP
Oxford University Press is a department of the University of Oxford.
It furthers the University's objective of excellence in research, scholarship,
and education by publishing worldwide in
Oxford New York

Athens Auckland Bangkok Bogotá Buenos Aires Calcutta
Cape Town Chennai Dar es Salaam Delhi Florence Hong Kong Istanbul
Karachi Kuala Lumpur Madrid Melbourne Mexico City Mumbai
Nairobi Paris São Paulo Singapore Taipei Tokyo Toronto Warsaw
and associated companies in Berlin Ibadan

Oxford is a registered trade mark of Oxford University Press
in the UK and certain other countries

Published in the United States
by Oxford University Press Inc., New York

©Zdeněk Stříbrný 2000

British Library Cataloguing in Publication Data
Data available

Library of Congress Cataloging-in-Publication Data
Stříbrný, Zdeněk.
  Shakespeare and Eastern Europe / Zdenek Stříbrny.
    p. cm.—(Oxford Shakespeare topics)
  Includes bibliographical references (p.) and index.
    1. Shakespeare, William, 1564–1616—Stage history—Europe, Eastern. 2. Shakespeare,
  William, 1564–1616—Appreciation—Europe, Eastern. 3. Shakespeare, William, 1564–1616—
  Stage history—Russia. 4. English drama–Appreciation—Europe, Eastern. 5. Russian literature—
  English influences. 6. English drama—Appreciation—Russia. 7. Slavic literature—English
  influences. 8.Theater—Europe, Eastern—History. 9. Europe, Eastern—Intellectual life.
    10. Theater—Russia—History. I. Title. II. Series.
  PR3109.E2 S52 2000   792.9′5′0947—dc21   99–048536
    ISBN 0-19-871165-4
    ISBN 0-19-871164-6 (pbk.)

10 9 8 7 6 5 4 3 2 1

Typeset by Kolam Information Services Pvt Ltd, Pondicherry, India
Printed in Great Britain
on acid-free paper by Biddles Ltd, Guildford and King's Lynn

My thanks are due to many people—my teachers, my colleagues, my students, librarians, archivists, actors, directors—and go far back. When I enrolled at Charles University in Prague after the Second World War, the most exciting class for me was Professor Otakar Vočadlo's seminar on Anglo-Russian literary relations. Under his stimulating supervision, I wrote my MA thesis on Shakespeare's influence on A. S. Pushkin. My second most important teacher was Professor Allardyce Nicoll at the Shakespeare Institute at Stratford-upon-Avon, where I was doing postgraduate research in a most inspiring community of scholars from all over the world.

Although my gratitude extends to a multitude of Shakespearian colleagues and friends, space forces me to mention only those who have directly helped me in writing this book. Reg Foakes came to Prague twice just in time to read and comment on the opening and closing chapters of my typescript; he also had the idea of providing the book with two maps of Eastern Europe. Lois Potter scrutinized some more chapters of my typescript and efficiently supplied me with photocopies of publications unavailable in Prague.

Some more Xeroxed materials from the British Library were sent to me by our London-based graduate student Jan Čáp. My former student, Dr Maxi Marysková, was my chief support at the National Library in Prague.

I have also received up-to-date information and materials from my good, reliable friends Marta Gibińska of the Jagiellonian University in Cracow, Alexander Shurbanov of the University of Sofia, and Jozef Olexa of Comenius University in Bratislava.

I have incurred great debts of gratitude to the two editors: Stanley Wells has read my script very carefully, correcting my mistakes or misprints and tightening up my style, while fully respecting my views with broad-minded generosity; Peter Holland has also been very generous, encouraging, and surprisingly knowledgeable about Slavonic matters. Furthermore, my Oxford press editor, Frances Whistler, has been very appreciative and sensitive in her suggestions for stylistic improvements and for trimming my script to the required word limit.

My wife Mariana has supported me all the time more than words can say.

Z.S.

Prague
July 1999

Contents

Maps and Illustrations

Map 1. The Holy Roman Empire and Eastern Europe in Shakespeare's T

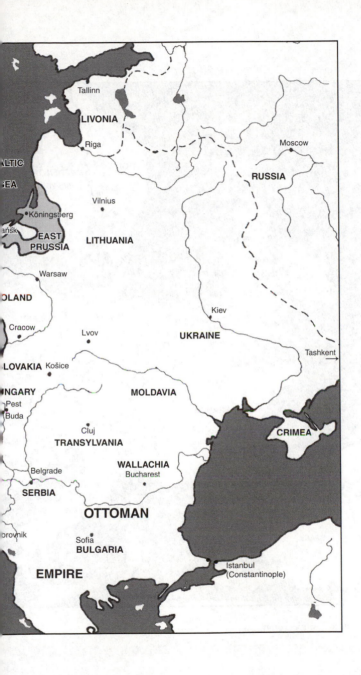

Map 2. Eastern Europe Today

Fig. 1. Pickleherring (1621)

In Eastern Europe, more than anywhere else, Shakespeare's plays have recently been appropriated for political interpretations, as will be shown in the latter parts of this book. Although such a topical approach to Shakespeare may be of special interest to the Western reader, I shall also try and explain how major East European poets, dramatists, novelists, translators, and critics, as well as actors, directors, designers, film-makers, composers, and other artists, have contributed to a better knowledge and appreciation of his work. The earliest example is the Prague engraver Wenceslaus Hollar (1607–77), whose drawings and etchings of seventeenth-century London have become an indispensable visual source for the modern reconstruction of Shakespeare's Globe, opened on the Bankside in Southwark in 1996–7. My intention is to give Eastern Europe its due and thus contribute to a fuller survey of Shakespeare's impact on the whole of Europe.

In discussing Eastern Europe, it will be useful to bear in mind that our present geographical notions and names are in many instances different from those of the age of Shakespeare (cf. Maps 1 and 2). At that time, the greatest power in Europe, the Holy Roman Empire of the German Nation, encompassed not only Germany and the Netherlands, part of Italy, and a piece of France but also many countries which are now considered to belong to Central or East Central Europe: for instance, the mostly Slavonic Kingdom of Bohemia (now the Czech Republic), the Archduchy of Austria, and the Archduchy of Styria (south Austria). The emperors were chosen by seven electors and crowned by the Pope until 1562 when their coronations started to take place without the Pope's blessing. The capital of the whole Empire from the fifteenth century was Vienna, but in the fourteenth century and again between 1583 and 1612 it was Prague.

Since 1438 the Empire had been ruled, with one exception, by the powerful dynasty of the Habsburgs of Austria whose family domain also included the western part of Hungary and almost the whole of Slovakia (now the Slovak Republic). Another branch of the Habsburgs, much better known in Shakespeare's England, ruled in Spain, large parts of Italy, the southern part of the Netherlands (now Belgium), Burgundy (now eastern France), and, since 1580, in Portugal, extending their domains to Mexico, Chile, Peru, Brazil, and even to the Philippines, named after King Philip II. The defeat of the Spanish 'Invincible Armada' by the English fleet in 1588 meant a decisive check to the Catholic Counter-Reformation in northern Europe and gave the main impetus to the outburst of the English national spirit which reverberates in Shakespeare's history plays.

Although the Habsburgs were growing increasingly absolutist and Catholic, in the Holy Roman Empire they had to concede various religious freedoms to Protestant electors and other nobles and wealthy citizens. Finally the Protestant Union was formed in 1608 under the leadership of the Calvinist Count Frederick, Elector Palatine. The Catholics were united in the Catholic League, founded in 1609 by Maximilian, Duke of Bavaria.

The long religious and political conflicts erupted in the anti-Habsburg uprising of the Bohemian Protestant estates (nobility, gentry, and bourgeoisie) starting the Thirty Years War (1618–48), the first all-European war, in which the Protestants were supported by Denmark, Sweden, the Protestant Netherlands, partly by England, and finally by France. The Habsburgs relied principally on the Catholic League, the Spanish Habsburgs, the Polish Vasas, and the Pope with his far-reaching influence. When the Peace of Westphalia was concluded, large parts of Germany and Bohemia lay in ruins. France and Sweden won important territories, and the sovereignty of the Protestant United Provinces of the Netherlands, the Swiss Confederation, and many German states, both larger and smaller, was recognized.

In the core of their domain (especially Bohemia and Austria), however, the Habsburgs restored the Catholic faith and absolutist order, transferring the confiscated lands of the Protestant Bohemian nobles and burghers to the Catholic aristocracy and officers of their imperial army. They continued to rule in what was finally called the Austro-Hungarian Monarchy until the end of the First World War.

Next to the Habsburgs, another strong European dynasty was the Vasas, who ruled in Sweden from 1523 and in Poland from 1587, when the Catholic Sigismund III of the Polish Vasa line became joint king of both countries. As he was more and more resented by the Protestant Swedes, he lost the Swedish crown in 1599. Thereafter the Catholic and Protestant branches of the Vasas were in conflict or open war until 1635 when Sigismund's son Vladislaus IV (ruled 1632–48) made peace between the Vasas. The Polish-Lithuanian state, created in 1569, was more than twice as large as present-day Poland, reaching from the Baltic to the Black Sea and including the Ukraine and Belarus.

Its eastern and south-eastern borders, however, were constantly disputed and attacked by the Russian tsars, especially Ivan IV, the Terrible (reigned 1547–84), whose cruel, autocratic measures extended the Russian Empire as far as western Siberia. At the same time, Ivan IV blocked the drives of the Tartars, thus making it possible for western and southern Europe to reach an unprecedented economic and cultural flowering. During the reign of the crafty and energetic Boris Godunov (1598–1605), who tried hard to defend tsarist territories on all sides, and especially after his tragic death, Russia experienced a 'Time of Troubles', marked by the appearance of usurpers, peasants' revolts, invasions from Poland and Sweden, and an interregnum (1610–13). The chaos was more or less ended by the accession of Michael I (1613–45) of the Romanov dynasty, which remained in power until the October Revolution in 1917.

Besides the East Slavs (the Russians, the Ukrainians, the Belarussians, etc.) and the West Slavs (the Poles, the Czechs, the Slovaks, etc.), the third large Slavonic population lived in south-east Europe on the Balkan Peninsula. These South Slavs (the Bulgarians, the Serbs, the Croats, the Montenegrins, the Slovenes) had formed several successive dukedoms and kingdoms in the Middle Ages but in Shakespeare's time they were subjected mostly to the Ottoman and partly to the Habsburg empires. The Ottoman Empire, as we can gather from *Othello*, loomed large as the most expansive power, reaching wide into Asia and Africa but also into south Europe. Sultan Suleyman I, the Magnificent (ruled 1520–66), brought most of the Balkan Peninsula under Turkish hegemony, including Bulgaria, Serbia, Bosnia, and Wallachia (now south Romania). In Transylvania (now north-west Romania) the Turks supported their vassals, the Protestant Hungarian nobles, in their struggles against the Catholic Habsburgs. The majority of the Hungarians, who were also tributary to the Sultan but were striving for independence, fought against both the Turks and the Habsburgs, but occasionally they concluded open or secret peace treaties on alternative sides. This policy seems to be reflected in the playful allusions to hungry peace in Shakespeare's *Measure for Measure* (1.2.1–5).

By the beginning of the twentieth century, the hegemony of the Ottoman Empire in south-east Europe was ended by two short Balkan wars. In the first war (1912–13), Serbia, Bulgaria, Greece, and Montenegro expelled Turkey from all its European possessions except for a small area around Constantinople (now Istanbul). In the second war (1913), Serbia, joined by Greece, Romania, and Turkey, forced Bulgaria to cede newly won territories to all four victors. The nationalism whipped up by the two Balkan wars was one of the causes of the First World War.

To cover such vast areas geographically and historically, it will be necessary to concentrate on the most crucial or the most controversial events in the individual East European countries and to bring only the most telling examples to life. Trying to do this, I shall rely primarily on my long experience of studying and watching Shakespeare behind the Iron Curtain or in the Cold (to use John le Carré's less hackneyed metaphor). Consequently, many of my examples will come from Prague in the hope that they will be not only firsthand but also representative enough for the whole extensive field. At the same time, I shall try to include as many parallels, or contrasts, from the other parts of Eastern Europe as possible.

While the fates of the individual East European countries have been extremely varied (springing from such greatly different ethnic and religious backgrounds as Slavonic, German, Hungarian, Romanian, Jewish, Muslim, Romany, etc.), some common features can also be observed, especially during the seven decades of the Soviet empire which was built with ruthless attempts at unification only to tumble down and splinter with astonishing speed. The chapters on Shakespeare under the Bolsheviks and behind the Iron Curtain prove the amazing adaptability of his plays to any political system but also the way his humanism can expose 'the whips and scorns of time', the 'oppressor's wrong', and the 'insolence of office'.[1]

FURTHER READING

A handy reference book is *A Concise Historical Atlas of Eastern Europe* by Dennis P. Hupchick and Harold E. Cox (New York, 1996). It presents maps of both larger and smaller parts of Eastern Europe in historical succession, with brief explanations of each. A few inaccurate or unclear details can be clarified by referring to items on individual countries, towns, and personalities in a reliable encyclopedia, e.g. *Encyclopaedia Britannica*, which has been continuously revised since its 14th edition (London, 1929). An admirable work of historical scholarship and a rich source of information about Central Europe in Shakespeare's time is *Rudolf II and his World: A Study in Intellectual History 1576–1612*, by R. J. W. Evans (Oxford, 1973, corrected paperback edn. 1984).

1

In the Beginning

I

Plays by Shakespeare and his fellow dramatists were already being staged in Eastern Europe during his lifetime. By the end of the sixteenth century, English actors had reached an unprecedented professional standard and, as their numbers were growing even in the face of Puritan opposition, they were looking for other places besides London to show their skills. Especially during plague epidemics and periods of sharp competition among acting companies, they went on tour not only in England and Scotland but also across the Channel. Their visits to the Continent represent one of the most intriguing chapters in the annals of British and European theatre.

Archival documents are scattered, tantalizingly brief, or lacking in more exact data. Nevertheless, the names of the principal actor-managers and popular clowns as well as the main routes of the English Comedians, as they were usually called, are known. We also have basic information about the staging of their plays, the stage properties and costumes, and the financial rewards they received. Several lists with the titles of their plays and some texts of the plays in German adaptations have survived. Evidently, the most attractive engagement for them was a long stay at the court of a rich aristocratic patron combined with shorter visits to the fairs and festivals of prosperous towns. They produced their plays in the halls of imperial, royal, or ducal palaces, fencing schools, town halls, town squares, inn-yards, or even churches and churchyards.

All the main genres of Elizabethan drama, i.e. comedies, romances, tragedies, and histories, were brought to the Continent. Moreover, a surprising number of old religious plays was also staged. Evidently, the strolling actors tried hard to satisfy pious patrons and citizens but also appealed to more secular and popular taste, so that they often enlivened their performances with additional jigs and acrobatics. Indignant protests against 'their jugglery, leaps, dances, songs and fantasies' have been preserved in a number of places in East Central Europe, supporting the chorus of Puritan voices in Germany and Britain itself. Sometimes the strollers were forbidden to continue their performances because they had shown 'disgraceful things', as in the east Prussian town of Elbing (Polish Elbląg) in 1606.[1]

Aristocratic patrons, on the other hand, tended to be much more permissive and sympathetic, as again in England. Even the pious young Archduchess Maria Magdalena of Styria (south Austria) praised ten performances at the Catholic archducal court in Graz in 1608, starting with *The Prodigal Son* and ending with another biblical play, *The Rich Man and Lazarus*, which was very pleasurable and moving, without 'the least bit of love-making in it'. The other performances were also 'vastly agreeable' or 'very enjoyable', with the exception of a 'terrifying play' about two brothers, *King Louis and King Frederick of Hungary*, 'with King Frederick stabbing and murdering everybody non-stop'.[2] Among the ten plays performed in Graz, probably two were by Marlowe, one by Dekker, and two were possibly related to Shakespeare's *Twelfth Night* and *The Merchant of Venice* respectively.

The most convenient way for the English Comedians to visit the Continent was through the Protestant part of the Netherlands or the Protestant Kingdom of Denmark. When the Earl of Leicester landed in Flushing in 1585 as commander of the English forces supporting the Dutch Protestants against the Spanish rulers of the Catholic part of the Netherlands, his entourage was enriched by several musicians and fifteen players, including the famous comedian Will Kemp. Leicester recommended his players to the King of Denmark, Frederick II, who had just completed a spacious, strongly fortified Renaissance castle, Kronborg, adjoining the port of Elsinore, a strategically vital entrance to the whole Baltic.

Of all places it is Elsinore (now Helsingør) which provides the first unquestionable records of English 'instrumentalists' and actors performing outside Britain. In 1585 they played in the courtyard of the town hall to a huge crowd of excited people and next year they returned, with Leicester's recommendation, to perform for several months at the royal castle. Among them were three men whose names were to appear as 'principal actors' in the First Folio edition of Shakespeare's collected plays (1623), including Will Kemp. Evidently, Shakespeare received first-hand information about Elsinore, Denmark, Norway, and Poland from his fellow actors.

From Denmark the English players apparently went to Germany in 1585 and again in 1586, probably without Kemp. In 1587 they possibly paid their first visit to Gdańsk, the key port for the so-called Baltic route which became much frequented by them in the first half of the seventeenth century, taking them along the sea-coast further east to Elbing, Königsberg (Kaliningrad), and Riga, or west to Stettin (Polish Szczecin), Wolgast, and Rostock.

The principal trailblazer of the English Comedians on the Continent was Robert Browne, who was in Leicester's entourage in the Netherlands in 1585, appeared again in Leiden in 1590, and continued to lead relays of actors on long tours mostly through Germany for about thirty years. In 1592 he gave performances at the court of Duke Henry Julius of Brunswick, a scholar and dramatist whose plays show the influence of Elizabethan drama. After staying at the Duke's residence at Wolfenbüttel until June 1592, Browne and his men went to perform at the autumn fair at Frankfurt am Main which had developed into the central European mart for the sale of cloth, wine, and many other articles, including books. The Frankfurt international fairs, held regularly in both spring and autumn, guaranteed appreciative and generous audiences so that they were visited by strolling players regularly for several decades.

The early performances of the English Comedians on the Continent were described by the Elizabethan traveller Fynes Moryson who watched both secular and religious productions by continental players in places as far apart as Leiden, Frankfurt, and Prague, comparing them to the visiting English professionals. He found the continental productions so 'dully penned, and worse acted' that 'when some of our cast [off] despised stage players came out of England into Germany, and played at Frankfurt in the time of the Mart, having neither a complete number of actors, nor any good apparel, nor any ornament of the stage, yet the Germans, not understanding a word they said, both men and women, flocked wonderfully to see their gesture and action'. A similarly enthusiastic response was received by the English Comedians at Leiden where 'many young virgins', according to Moryson's gossipy anticipation of modern groupies, 'fell in love with some of the players, and followed them from city to city till the magistrates were forced to forbid them to play any more'.[3]

Although Moryson's comments appear harsh and puritanical, he was undoubtedly right in observing that the English Comedians impressed continental audiences not by the power of their words, which could not be understood, but by their physical action and additional jigs and the high jumps of the tumbler, accompanied by plenty of music. Gradually, however, the English companies also employed German and Dutch actors, becoming more and more international and playing more and more in German. They were also able to adapt themselves to the different religious creeds of their patrons, not excepting the Catholic faith of the Habsburgs.

The most important patron of Robert Browne and other English actors proved to be Maurice of Hesse, a learned Calvinist, who maintained acting troupes for long periods at his court in Kassel where he finally, in 1611, built a spacious theatre called the Ottoneum. Browne was in Kassel as early as 1594 or 1595. In 1596 the Landgrave wrote to his agent in Prague asking him to give assistance to his comedians in case of their visit to that city. Obviously, Browne and his men had to supplement the Landgrave's hospitality with further income gained by touring vast territories in and outside Germany, going as far as Prague and possibly even Gdańsk.

Apparently the most adventurous and adaptable of all the strollers who joined Robert Browne on the Continent was John Green. He had won a reputation for playing first virgins and wives and later on jolly clowns. It was probably thanks to him that the popular comic character called Pickleherring was introduced to the Continent. Green's name first emerged in Browne's company in 1603 in Lille, which was then within the Spanish Netherlands ruled by the Habsburgs. After performing with Browne in Ghent, Paris, Lille again, and Strasbourg, he separated from his master in Frankfurt in 1607 and struck out with his own group far into new territories in the east, as distant from each other as Gdańsk on the Baltic Sea and Graz in south Austria. According to indirect but convincing evidence, he was the principal actor of the company who performed at the Catholic court of the Styrian Habsburgs in Graz in 1608, as discussed above.

After an extended return to the Spanish Netherlands, Green's troupe made another long journey to Gdańsk in 1612 to play at the newly built wooden public arena, the so-called Fencing School. Gdańsk was a populous and wealthy international port and trade centre with arguably the largest English colony on the Continent. The erection of the spacious arena was an additional attraction for strolling players who visited it frequently for two or more weeks, with special attention to the traditional St Dominic Fair in August.

Thanks to the vision and initiative of the Polish scholar and writer Jerzy Limon of Gdańsk University, a new foundation has been formed, Theatrum Gedanense, whose goal it is to reconstruct a Shakespearian theatre on the historic site of the original playhouse. A special feature of the Gdańsk theatre will be its rectangular design, copied from an old engraving by a Dutch artist, Peter Willer, first printed in 1687.[4] The original structure depicted by Willer, which differs from the round or polygonal shape of the Globe, was probably modelled on London's Fortune, the chief rival of Shakespeare's theatre from 1600 until 1621. Meanwhile, a fairly exact replica of the Globe itself—a simple but attractive wooden structure built by modern technology—has been opened in a large amusement park in Prague (on 21 July 1999) with a Czech version of *Romeo and Juliet*. The name of the new theatre, Globe '99, alludes to the fact that the original London Globe was opened exactly 400 years ago. Thus, following the lead of the new London Globe, there will be theatres in Slavonic Europe in which Shakespeare's plays can be staged in conditions similar to those in his own time.

In 1615 Green's company revisited Gdańsk from Wolfenbüttel and in 1616 they were back again, this time by sea from Denmark. Their usual petition asking the city authorities for permission to perform was signed, on behalf of all the group, by both John Green and a new actor. He was Robert Reynolds, Robert Browne's son-in-law, later to stand out as jester and leader of his own company. From Gdańsk, Green and Co. went to Warsaw but soon they undertook a long tour to other places, such as Olomouc (German Olmütz, in Moravia), Vienna, and Prague. In 1617 spectacular festivities took place in Prague, celebrating the proclamation of Ferdinand II of Styria as the future king of

Bohemia. The old and ailing Emperor Matthias came to Prague in person to persuade the predominantly Protestant estates into accepting the Habsburg succession after his death.

As a relief from the tense political negotiations, a masque of great formality and scenic splendour was performed by the foremost Bohemian and Moravian noblemen dressed in highly mannerist costumes. The most spectacular feature was saved for the ending, when all the participants paid a solemn tribute to an allegorical female figure hovering high up in the clouds and representing the Habsburg House of Fame. Moreover, at least one English and one German professional company played during the festivities. According to the Emperor's register of expenses, 'John Green of London' was paid 200 florins.

Despite all the glory and the power, the strictly Catholic and absolutist Habsburgs were growing increasingly unpopular in largely Protestant and Slavonic Bohemia, and in 1619, after the death of Emperor Matthias, the Bohemian estates refused Ferdinand II as king of Bohemia and elected instead Frederick, Elector Palatine of the Rhine, the leader of the Protestant Union. One of their political aims was to win the support of Great Britain, since Frederick was the husband of Elizabeth, daughter of James I. During their betrothal celebrations in London in 1613 a number of plays had been produced, almost half of them by Shakespeare. Therefore it is perhaps not too fanciful to suggest that Frederick and Elizabeth, who were both patrons of London theatre companies, might have brought about an early flowering of genuine Shakespearian drama in East Central Europe.

At all events, they invited the most experienced and distinguished continental stroller Robert Browne to come to Prague during his fifth and last tour. When he started the tour in 1618, he was most probably well informed about the activities of other English strollers on the Continent, and some collaboration or even temporary fusion with them can be supposed. We know for certain that Robert Reynolds, who had been with Green at Gdańsk in 1616, played with his father-in-law Browne at Strasbourg and possibly also at Frankfurt in 1618. Some scholars have speculated that it was the combined Browne–Green concern which visited Rostock and Gdańsk in July 1619 before going to Prague.

Although no direct records of this visit have been preserved, we can assume that Browne's company came to celebrate the coronation of

Frederick and Elizabeth at Prague Castle in November 1619 and possibly also the birth of their son Rupert at the very end of the year. King James I, however, remained lukewarm in the Bohemian cause, although many of his subjects were in sympathy with it and some, from both England and Scotland, went to Bohemia as volunteers in the Protestant army, supported by the Water Poet John Taylor and his verses 'An Englishman's Love to Bohemia'.

But the defeat of the Protestants at the battle of White Mountain near Prague in November 1620 forced Frederick and his wife to take flight and thus for a long time to bury Czech hopes of an independent political, religious, and cultural life. While the royal couple were called the 'Winter King and Queen of Bohemia', in remembrance of their only Bohemian winter of 1619–20, the Czech lands were exposed to Counter-Reformation and Germanization by the victorious Habsburg Emperor and King Ferdinand II. In England, the Elector Palatine's or Palsgrave's Men were active from 1612 until 1625 and the Queen of Bohemia's Men (formerly Lady Elizabeth's Men) played at least until 1632. By that time, Elizabeth presided over her 'Court of Bohemia' in The Hague, where she and her husband found their final refuge.

Robert Browne's men returned from Prague via Nuremberg to Frankfurt in March 1620 for the Easter fair. They were first refused permission to perform because of 'the dangerous course of war events' but finally their supplication was granted in view of the 'always unobjectionable' behaviour of their master. This is the last but telling piece of information we have about Robert Browne on the Continent.

II

John Green seems to have taken his men home to England in 1620 but in 1624 he appeared again in Ghent and then at the court of the Elector of Saxony, John George I, in Dresden and Torgau in 1626–7. A thorough catalogue of plays has been preserved from Dresden, listing forty-two performances between 31 May and 4 December 1626. If we compare this catalogue to the older survey of Green's performances at Graz in 1608, we notice that eight titles are identical but many new items are added. The most remarkable among the new items are *The Tragedy of Romeo and Juliet*, *The Tragedy of Julius Caesar*, *The Tragedy of*

Hamlet, Prince of Denmark, The Tragedy of Lear, King of England, and again *The Tragedy of Romeo and Juliet.* These are the first recorded performances of *Julius Caesar* and *King Lear* on the Continent. Two more of the listed items call for closer attention: *The Comedy of Joseph, the Jew of Venice,* which was probably based to some extent on *The Merchant of Venice,* and *The Tragicomedy of the Clever Thief,* which has been suspected of having some relation to the character of Autolycus in *The Winter's Tale.* The latter play was evidently most appealing, as it was performed three times during the Dresden festivities. The striking increase in Shakespearian repertoire can be best explained in connection with the publication of the First Folio in 1623, which made Shakespeare's plays easily available to all companies. This may be particularly the case with *Julius Caesar* and *The Winter's Tale,* which were published in the Folio for the first time and soon became very popular in Germany and East Central Europe.

From Dresden Green and his men took the risk of travelling to Nuremberg but were not permitted to perform there. Falling back on the route of their old master Browne they went on to Frankfurt, the strollers' paradise. There they received the badly needed permission to play during the autumn fair of 1627. As in the case of Browne, no more records have been discovered on Green after Frankfurt.

As the Thirty Years War was dragging on, those English actors who remained on the Continent were looking eastward for safer places. The most attractive refuge for them was offered by the royal court in Warsaw, where John Green's men had already performed in 1617 before going on the long tour to Prague. In the same year and again in 1618 Green's companion George Vincent was sent by the Prince of Poland, Vladislaus, to bring new supplies of performers and theatre materials directly from London, as attested by two passports granted to him by the Privy Council for his return to Poland. The most remarkable among the acquisitions was Richard Jones, a well-known London actor and a seasoned stroller who first visited the Continent with Browne as early as 1589. This time Jones evidently decided to settle in Warsaw for a longer stay because his wife joined him in 1618 with George Vincent's second expedition.

Since the King of Poland, Sigismund III, remained more or less neutral during the Central European war and his son and successor Vladislaus IV concluded a separate peace with Sweden in 1635, the court in Warsaw acquired an unusual importance for all artists. Unfortunately, most of the archive materials in Warsaw were destroyed during the numerous wars that devastated the country, and the rest of the collection of old records was burned in an air raid in the Second World War. In spite of that, it is clear that English actors became permanently attached to the Warsaw royal court not only between 1616 and 1620 but also in the periods about 1628–32 and 1636–44, or even longer. In 1637 King Vladislaus IV opened a theatre hall within the royal castle, designed by the Italian architect Agostino Locci for productions of Italian operas. Here English Comedians found a technically developed stage and a new source of inspiration for their own performances to become more elaborate and visually impressive. They could make good use of the changeable scenery, illusionistic decorations, serious music, and complex machinery. Apart from finding refuge from the horrors of the Thirty Years War, they could experiment in new trends of European staging.

In comparison, similar attempts in England were hampered by the Civil War and the closing of public theatres by the Puritans in 1642. The royalist theatre manager William Davenant was imprisoned several times during the Commonwealth period, with the result that he could fully develop his activities only after the Stuart Restoration in 1660 when his adaptations of Shakespeare, operatic in scenery and neoclassicist in diction, were applauded by the London audiences, who were now smaller and less socially representative.

Besides the royal court in Warsaw and the city of Gdańsk, which belonged to the Polish crown as part of what was called Royal Prussia, the most appealing place for the English Comedians was Königsberg (now Kaliningrad), another Baltic sea-port and trade centre with a rich cultural and intellectual life. The University of Königsberg, founded in 1544, reached its highest reputation thanks to such professors as Immanuel Kant in the eighteenth century or Alexander Schmidt, whose *Shakespeare-Lexicon*, published in 1874–5 and reprinted many times, has remained one of the most useful reference books for translators all over the world.

In Shakespeare's time, Königsberg was the capital of so-called Ducal Prussia (later known as East Prussia) which was ruled by the electors of Brandenburg, who belonged to the mighty Hohenzollern dynasty. That is why the 'dukes in Prussia', although they were vassals of the kings of Poland, were able to maintain a good deal of independence. In 1525 Ducal Prussia became the first Lutheran state in Europe and in 1613 it was converted to Calvinism, in sharp contrast to the Catholic Vasas in Warsaw. Rather than in small and provincial Berlin, the electors of Brandenburg often preferred to reside at their impressive castle at Königsberg, where they could entertain their guests in the 'Old Great Hall', which was also used for musical and theatrical performances.

The most striking figure among the English Comedians patronized by the electors of Brandenburg was John Spencer, who headed his company from at least 1604, performing plays in Berlin, Königsberg, Gdańsk, Elbing, probably Warsaw, and many places in Germany and the Netherlands. He played for Protestant nobles and citizens, both Lutheran and Calvinist, as well as for Catholic audiences, including Emperor Matthias. He and his men had to turn their coats quickly not only in the theatre but also in real life. According to Catholic sources, Spencer, his wife and children, and all his actors were miraculously turned from Protestantism 'to their true mother the Catholic church' by a Franciscan friar in Cologne in 1615. It is difficult to judge from this distance how far their conversion was sincere and durable. Spencer was active until about 1623 and became widely popular as a clown called Hans Leberwurst (i.e. Liverwurst) and later Hans Stockfish.

Several times he and his company visited Pomerania, a west Baltic region, which was (like Brandenburg) part of the Empire. It was ruled by the dynasty of the Greifens who were Slavonic in origin but Germanized through long political and personal relations with the Duchy of Brandenburg. One of the enlightened Greifens, Duke Philip Julius, paid two visits to London and in 1602 he attended several performances by both adult and boy actors. Back at home, he repeatedly invited strolling English Comedians to his court at Wolgast, recommending them for performances at other Pomeranian towns, especially Stettin (Polish Szczecin), the capital of East Pomerania. Besides John Spencer's men, whose longer visits to Pomerania can be traced from 1606, it was Richard Jones and his companions who found employment, after their four-year service at the royal court in Warsaw (1617–20), at the ducal court at Wolgast in 1622 and possibly again in 1624.

The first collection of the English Comedians' plays published in Germany in 1620 and again in 1624 probably also came from Pomerania. It was entitled *Engelische Comedien und Tragedien* and its German is clearly tinged with Low German dialect interspersed with many Anglicisms. The editorship of the plays was claimed by Friedrich Menius, a practising lawyer in Wolgast, who probably attended the performances of the English players at the court of Duke Philip Julius, noting and memorizing the text and reconstructing the plays on the basis of his notes. He may also have procured some texts from the English Comedians themselves, especially from those who were preparing to return to England as the continental war was breaking out.

Highly interesting and amusing as these German prose versions are, from both the linguistic and the theatrical point of view, they are a far cry from the English originals, as far as we know them. They give us a good idea of how drastically the English plays were garbled in the process of adaptation to the particular demands of continental audiences. Out of the eight plays and seven farces and jigs printed in this collection, two are related to Shakespeare. *Julio and Hyppolita* echoes the name of Shakespeare's Queen of the Amazons from *A Midsummer Night's Dream* for the title heroine, but the action reveals more resemblance to *The Two Gentlemen of Verona*. Closer to Shakespeare is *The Most Lamentable Tragedy of Titus Andronicus*, and it is certainly significant that the only preserved copy of the First Quarto of Shakespeare's tragedy, printed in 1594, was discovered in 1904 as far away as Sweden, very close to Pomerania. Another surprising discovery in those far-off regions was the seventh extant copy of the Second Quarto of *Hamlet* (dated 1605) which was unearthed in 1950 in the University Library of Wrocław (German Breslau), the capital of Silesia.

When the peace treaty between Poland and Sweden was signed in 1635, ending the war that started in 1626, exceptionally favourable conditions were offered to English Comedians by the Polish Kingdom and the Duchy of Prussia until about 1655, when a new war, known in Poland as the Swedish 'Deluge', broke out. Between 1636 and 1644 in particular the cultural triangle Warsaw–Gdańsk–Königsberg was highly frequented. At least two actor-managers active there at that time deserve special mention: Robert Archer who, according to his own statement, served the King of Poland 'for many years', and Robert Reynolds. The latter was, as mentioned above, the son-in-law of

Robert Browne, an associate of John Green, and leader of the Elector of Saxony's players in the late 1620s. He built up his reputation as a widely popular comedian playing the part of Pickleherring.

According to the lively account of another English traveller, Peter Mundy, who visited Denmark, Russia, and Prussia in the years 1639– 48 and stopped at Gdańsk in 1642, Reynolds's Pickleherring was much talked of and admired because he 'could so Frame his Face and countenance that to one half of the people on the one side he would seem heartily to laugh and to those on the other side bitterly to weep and shed tears'.[5] Mundy has also preserved the valuable information that Reynolds died in Warsaw shortly after 1640 and his wife was awarded an 'allowance' by the Polish King for her 'maintenance' in the city of Gdańsk. The support of the Polish royal court for English Comedians was so renowned that they sometimes introduced themselves, when they went on tours through Germany, as the Polish Comedians. More popularly, they advertised themselves as 'Pickleherring's company'.

III

Since Pickleherring became so exceptionally popular, a brief enquiry into his origin and development seems to be pertinent. In the *Oxford English Dictionary* 'Pickle-herring' is defined (under 2) as 'A clown, a buffoon, a merry-andrew' with the addition that this application originated in German and not in English as Grimm's Dictionary had stated. Another etymological explanation, shared by Joseph Addison, supposed that Pickleherring was first a Dutch comic character. This view seems to be supported by art historians who have observed that in some Flemish illuminated manuscripts of the fifteenth century a herring was placed over the Fool's cap as an emblem of folly. More substantial evidence, however, can be found in the English medieval Sword Play preserved at Revesby, in which the Fool and his 'first son' Pickle Herring are the chief leaders of all the dancing, singing, jumping, and playing with swords.[6]

Recent research tends to confirm that the name and the fame of Pickleherring were spread by the English Comedians, especially John Green, George Vincent, and Robert Reynolds. In print, Pickleherring appeared quite prominently on the extensive title-page of the *Engelische*

Comedien und Tragedien of 1620 which introduced him among the chief characters and presented him as the protagonist of two of the additional farces and jigs. In one of them, entitled *A Merry Pickleherring Play about Beautiful Maria and Old Henry*, the title heroine lived in Gdańsk at the 'Long Market', which can still be visited today in the Old Town of the city.

Such topical allusions were abundant in ballads and broadsides about Pickleherring and his adventures in East Central Europe. A broadside published in 1621 is adorned with a striking engraving of Pickleherring wearing a long doublet with big buttons, loose hose, large boots that could be kicked at his adversary, and a smart cap decorated with a fox brush as a sign of his cunning. His face, embellished with a bristling moustache, is half in bright light and half in darkness. Over his shoulder he is carrying a huge pedlar's pack overloaded with broad axes, while more axes are lying on the ground or resting in his arms, including one that is almost as big as himself. In the accompanying text Pickleherring explains that he has given up acting to become an ironmonger and now he is hurrying to Prague to sell his broad axes to the Bohemian heretics and iconoclasts. It is remarkable how quickly the Catholic propagandists appropriated Pickleherring for their satirical attacks against the image-breaking zeal of the defeated Protestants, as soon as the Calvinist Winter King was obliged to leave Bohemia to its fate.

In Elizabethan England, pickleherring–Pickleherring seems to have been a common fare both in real life and on the stage. The notoriously dissolute writer Robert Greene was rumoured to have died after a meal in which he had overindulged in wine and pickled herring. Similarly, the brilliant stylist Thomas Nashe was commiserated with for having 'shortened his days by keeping company with pickle herrings'. In Marlowe's *Doctor Faustus* Peter Pickle-herring is identified as one of the godfathers of Gluttony. Shakespeare's Sir Toby Belch wishes a plague upon 'pickle herring' that make him belch in the morning (*Twelfth Night*, 1.5.116–17). It may be significant that Sir Toby's curse comes exactly at the moment when the clown Feste first appears in the play. Later on (3.1.32–3), Feste jokes that 'fools are as like husbands as pilchards are to herrings' (in A. Schmidt's *Shakespeare-Lexicon* Pilcher=pilchard is defined as 'a fish of the genus Clupea, much resembling the herring'). These puzzling allusions in *Twelfth*

Night seem to hint at some connection between 'pickle herring' and the fool, between the 'corrupter of words' Feste and Pickleherring who, in the performances of the English Comedians, was twisting words in both English and German.

Perhaps the most remarkable parallel to the Pickleherring of the English Comedians can be seen in the Bohemian rogue Autolycus, Shakespeare's most original creation in *The Winter's Tale*, where the tide of the romance turns from the obsessed violence of the Sicilian court to the entirely fictitious sea-coast and countryside of pastoral Bohemia. From his first entrance (4.3), Autolycus, more frequently than Feste, arrests the attention of the audience by his songs, as did Pickleherring on the Continent, the more so that the other English players could not be understood by foreign audiences.

From the time of the early tours of the English Comedians the clown, who was expected to learn foreign languages quickly, formed the chief link between the actors and the spectators, introducing other characters and commenting on the action. It is certainly interesting that in the new Oxford edition of *The Winter's Tale* Autolycus' essential function is also described as bridging 'the gap between stage and audience'.[7] To strengthen the bridge and get the laughs and applause of the spectators both Autolycus and Pickleherring, like other clowns, used asides and, even more frequently, bawdy and body language, full of sexual allusions. We hear from the joking servant that Autolycus' songs fit both men and women of all sizes and that 'the prettiest love songs for maids' are 'without bawdry', which is strange because they include such burdens as 'jump her and thump her'. The Bohemian princely shepherdess Perdita can see through all this farcical nonsense and asks the servant bluntly to forewarn Autolycus 'that he use no scurrilous words in's tunes' (4.4.214–15). It is worth remembering that about the same time the young Austrian Archduchess Maria Magdalena found the English Comedians in Graz perfectly decent, evidently to counterbalance moralistic complaints about their obscenity.

In his opening song, Autolycus enthuses over 'a quart of ale' as 'a dish for a king', displaying the most pronounced feature of Pickleherring: his obsession with food and drink. Revealing his own *curriculum vitae* (4.3.85–98), Autolycus states that, among many other employments and activities, he went about with the puppet show of the Prodigal Son. This reminds us of the continental comedians' repertory in which the biblical play of the same title was used to win the favour of devout patrons. When Autolycus re-enters (4.4.218) wearing a false beard as his 'pedlar's excrement' and carrying his pedlar's pack, he calls forth the image of the mustachioed and overloaded Pickleherring hurrying to Bohemia with his hardware of axes, sharply different from Autolycus' software of sheets, ribbons, laces, and gloves. Advertising one of his sensational printed ballads as being 'very true, and but a month old', Autolycus resembles Pickleherring involved in the most topical religious and political events of the day.

Finally the dance of the twelve 'men of hair' who are both 'saltiers' (i.e. leapers) and satyrs (*The Winter's Tale*, 4.4.324–40) is reminiscent of the exploits of the English tumbler or leaper who became a great favourite with the merry wives and virgins of Frankfurt, as described in a racy German poem printed in 1597:

> The tumbler also did us please,
> He sprang high in the air with ease.
> In dancing he had not a peer,
> A joy it was to see him near.
> His hose they fitted him so tight,
> His codpiece was a lovely sight.
> Nubile maids and lecherous dames
> He kindled into lustful flames.[8]

All this persuades me to see *The Winter's Tale*, and especially Autolycus, as an illuminating parallel to the ways used by English Comedians in applying their native traditions and patterns of comic acting to their productions on the Continent. By an uncanny historical coincidence it was this Sicilian–Bohemian romance which was selected as one of the fourteen plays to be performed for King James's daughter Elizabeth and her fiancé the Elector Palatine during the two months of celebrations preceding their London marriage in 1613. By that time rumours were circulating at the royal court about the bridegroom's expectations of being crowned King of Bohemia within a few years.

Sometimes individual scenes were picked up from all over Shakespeare and adapted for Pickleherring farces or inserted into other plays to which Pickleherring was added. Autolycus' tricks can serve again as an example, as his knack for picking the pockets of credulous Bohemian rustics was freely imitated. The demand of continental audiences for Pickleherring was so insatiable that he had to be introduced even into tragedies. This, of course, did not go against the grain of Elizabethan and Shakespearian drama. The difference was not so much in quantity as in quality: Shakespeare's Fool in *King Lear* easily surpasses all continental Pickleherrings by the subtlety of his wit and the significance of the role he plays in the structure of the tragedy.

Perhaps the best example of Pickleherring's extended role is the adaptation of *Romeo and Juliet* which was first performed on the Continent, as far as we know, in 1604, and survived to score a great success after the Thirty Years War. As soon as the Peace of Westphalia was finally signed in 1648, English Comedians started to revisit their favourite haunts in Germany and East Central Europe with added vigour, the more so as the revolutionary Parliament in London passed a harsh order in February 1648, branding stage players as rogues punishable by fines, imprisonment, and public flogging. Frequent visits of English Comedians in the post-war period are recorded in Vienna, Prague, and Gdańsk. Some new places are also added to their routes, such as Innsbruck (west Austria) and Bratislava (the present capital of Slovakia). When *Romeo and Juliet* was performed in Prague in 1658 at a high-society banquet, it prompted a curious yet typical note in the diary of the Archbishop of Prague. Leaving aside the star-crossed lovers, he singled out for his praise Pickleherring, 'who was very good and funny'.[9]

The Court Library of Vienna holds a manuscript of a German version of *Romeo and Juliet* dating from the second half of the seventeenth century and bearing unmistakable allusions to a number of towns in south Bohemia and north Austria.[10] The most conspicuous features of the play, however, are the general deterioration of language, crammed with obscenities and banal clichés, as well as the special stress laid on the horrors of war. Instead of Shakespeare's Prologue and the scuffling scene between the servants of the Capulets and the Montagues, a formal opening is provided for with the Prince condemning 'war and devastation', when 'one race is destroying the other' and common people are 'bleeding from the heavy yoke' of the enmity. Immediately, peace is concluded with great pomp and highfalutin speeches from Mundige (Montague) and the Prince. Starting where Shakespeare ends, the German version never gains the growing tension of Shakespeare's tragedy. Nor does it capture Romeo's and

Juliet's growth in individuality and the intensity and passion of their love.

Easily the liveliest but also the crudest scenes are dominated by Pickleherring, who is developed from the minor part of Shakespeare's clownish servant Peter and also steals some saucy bits from the Nurse. When Juliet is advised by the Nurse to 'leave perjured Romeo' and take Count Paris for her husband, Pickleherring prods the young heroine to have them both and, moreover, take himself for her bridegroom, too: 'Has not the Turkish Emperor more wives than one can count? Why should it not be permitted to take 3, 4, 5, 6, 7, 8, 9 or 10 wives or husbands? I should not have far to go if in Kollschin, Budweiss, Gopplitz, Freystadt, Linz, and in this town I would find out husbands or wives who desire, nay who have, more than one wife or husband.'

Pickleherring cracks jokes over the very corpses of Tybalt, whom he calls 'a parcel of snot...bleeding like a pig', and of Juliet, who is 'stretched out like a log' and appears to him 'as stiff as a frozen stockfish'. The ending of the German adaptation is highly didactic and religious: Capulet and the Friar warn against the imprudence of youth and the destructiveness of love, while the Prince offers consolation in faith in an afterlife:

> What Heaven may take here, again can Heaven give,
> We must remember that we shall for ever live.

Pickleherring's all-pervasive popularity can be finally confirmed by further pictorial evidence. In a Silesian edition of the widely disseminated language textbook *Orbis sensualium pictus* (1667) by the Moravian humanist and educational reformer J. A. Comenius, an engraving of a stage performance shows Pickleherring strutting and dramatically gesticulating at other characters in the reconciliation scene of *The Prodigal Son*. Comenius had to leave Bohemia after the defeat of the Protestants and live in exile, residing in England in 1641–2. He was not only the first to use pictures systematically in the teaching of languages but conceived of the whole educational process as a play inspiring pupils to creative participation, as in his cycle of school dramas entitled *Schola ludus*, first published in Hungary (1656) and in Amsterdam (1657).

The painted backcloth and wings as well as the baroque curtain represented in the Silesian engraving remind us that the continental stages were progressing, under the influence of court masques, Italian opera, and French pastorals, towards more and more elaborate sets. The most energetic exponent of the new trends in continental staging in the period about 1646–60 was George Jolly (alias Joris Jolliphus), one of the last major English Comedians. Jolly is well known in the annals of English theatre as a dangerous rival of Sir William Davenant and Thomas Killigrew, the two Restoration courtiers who tried hard to assert their theatrical monopoly after 1660. Before that Jolly had become so successful on the Continent that in 1654 he could advertise his performances as offering 'good instructive stories...repeated changes of expensive costumes, and a theatre decorated in the Italian manner, with beautiful English music and skilful women'.[11]

As far as we know, Jolly was the first of the English actor-managers to bring women upon the boards. Although he was, according to available evidence, a violent, rapacious, and unscrupulous manager, ready to use his fists in asserting his authority or discouraging competition, he has been acknowledged as 'the first English producer to use the modern stage'. His greatest successes on the Continent were scored in Frankfurt, where his performances were visited by Charles II with his exiled courtiers in 1655. This gave Master Jolly and his company the opportunity to style themselves 'The King's Servants'. They also played during the coronation of Emperor Leopold I at Frankfurt in 1658, embellishing their repertory with the evergreen *Prodigal Son*.

Given Jolly's adventurous spirit, it is not surprising to find his company, sometimes fused with some other strolling group, visiting such far-off and dispersed places as Gdańsk, Stockholm, Vienna, Nuremberg, Basle, and Cologne. His performances in 1659 shocked the traditionally conservative Viennese public by being 'spiced with the most scandalous obscenities'. At the beginning of 1660 he was expelled from Nuremberg because of a violent quarrel. All this must have prompted Master Jolly to think of returning home to cash in on his acquaintance with King Charles II whose restoration was in the air as much on the continent as in England.

The early reception of Shakespeare and other Elizabethan dramatists in East Central Europe proved that their plays were unusually adaptable to any geographical location, staging condition, social milieu, and religio-political situation. The high professional standard of the

English Comedians was appreciated, with predictable exceptions, at the imperial, royal, and ducal courts in Vienna, Graz, Prague, Warsaw, or Königsberg, at the international fairs of thriving commercial centres such as Gdańsk, and at many other larger or smaller towns in Austria, Bohemia, Moravia, Slovakia, Silesia, Poland, Prussia, Pomerania, or Livonia. The popularity of the comic characters, particularly Pickleherring, was so great that they were incorporated not only into many comedies but also into tragedies and, in special adaptations, into puppet shows. There is a record of 'merry English figures' shown in Prague in 1666–7. Such puppet shows also continued to attract popular audiences much further east down to the eighteenth and nineteenth centuries. For instance, a puppet play about Doctor Faustus was performed in Moscow in 1761. In short, the impact of the English Comedians in Central and Eastern Europe was very strong and lasting, inspiring the development of the native theatre in its entire artistic and social gamut reaching from the grass roots of popular theatricals up to the royal and imperial courts.

FURTHER READING

A basic book is Albert Cohn's *Shakespeare in Germany in the Sixteenth and Seventeenth Centuries* (London, 1865, repr. Wiesbaden, 1967). The subtitle gives a succinct description of the contents: *An Account of English Actors in Germany and the Netherlands and of the Plays Performed by Them during the Same Period*; in addition, German adaptations of Shakespeare's *Titus Andronicus*, *Hamlet*, and *Romeo and Juliet* are presented both in the original and in English translations. Five early German Shakespearian adaptations translated into English are introduced and edited by Ernest Brennecke, *Shakespeare in Germany, 1590–1700* (Chicago, 1964): besides the adaptations of *Titus Andronicus* and *Hamlet* very free offshoots of *A Midsummer Night's Dream*, *The Merchant of Venice*, and *Twelfth Night* are included. E. K. Chambers's *The Elizabethan Stage*, 4 vols. (Oxford, 1923) has a chapter on 'International Companies' with a sub-chapter on 'English Players on the Continent' in vol. ii. Chambers's work was continued by G. E. Bentley, *The Jacobean and Caroline Stage*, 7 vols. (Oxford, 1941–68) and Leslie Hotson, *The Commonwealth and Restoration Stage* (Cambridge, Mass., 1928). Some of Cohn's and Chambers's errors were corrected and new facts were presented by Willem Schrickx in two articles in *Shakespeare Survey*, 33 (1980) and 36 (1983). The latter essay supplies valuable information about Pickleherring. New documents about the English

Comedians in Poland and the whole Baltic area were published and discussed in a broad context by Jerzy Limon, *Gentlemen of a Company: English Players in Central and Eastern Europe, 1590–1660* (Cambridge, 1985). Current English scholarship is represented by Andrew Gurr, *The Shakespearian Playing Companies* (Oxford, 1996). Recent American research is presented by Simon Williams in his illustrated *Shakespeare on the German Stage*, i: *1586–1914* (Cambridge, 1990). A number of books on the subject have been written in German. Even those who do not read German can have a look at Emil Herz, *Englische Schauspieler und englisches Schauspiel zur Zeit Shakespeares in Deutschland* (Hamburg, 1903) because it contains five maps showing the routes of different companies of English strollers all over Europe.

2

Shakespeare under the Tsars

I

Although English Comedians, unlike the merchants, did not venture upon tours to Russia, their acting skills and some of their texts were brought by their German successors as far as Moscow and other places of the vast tsarist empire. The reputation of the English strollers was so unrivalled that the trademark 'English Comedians' was often used also by German wandering actors. Among them, Pickleherring ruled the roost as usual in jigs, comedies, as well as tragedies. In a Russian play called *Bajazed and Tamerlan* (acted between 1672 and 1676), roughly derived from Marlowe's *Tamburlaine the Great*, the blood-thirsty conflict between two oriental tyrants was alleviated by Pickle-herring's gags and gimmicks in which the play's cynical and farcical elements were concentrated. Russian variations on Pickleherring continued to appear until about the 1720s.

The first tsar to emulate Western and East Central European rulers in establishing a court theatre was Alexis Mikhailovitch, who patron-ized an acting company for about four years before his death in 1676. When Peter I, the Great (ruled 1682–1725), returned from his Grand Tour in Europe, he had a wooden theatre built on the big Moscow square, the so-called 'Red Square', right by the Kremlin Palace. The first company to perform there came from Gdańsk in 1702 with a German repertory, but Russian disciples were trained at the same time. After Peter's decision to move his court to St Petersburg in 1707, the Moscow theatre was pulled down, and Russian performances, under the patronage of the Tsar's youngest sister Natalya Alexeevna, were opened in the new metropolis to a broad public who were granted free admission. The chief dramatic model was Molière, but the now-ennobled 'Prince Pikel Giering' was still standing his ground.

In the middle of the eighteenth century, the first Russian adaptation of Shakespeare was played at the Imperial Theatre in St Petersburg. It was *Hamlet*, or *Gamlet* as it is called in Russian (printed 1748, performed 1850), by Alexander Sumarokov (1718–77), the first Russian nobleman who devoted himself to writing poetry, prose, and plays professionally. His most important contribution to the development of Russian literature was the introduction of verse into tragedy. His *Gamlet*, the second of his nine tragedies, was probably inspired by a recent French translation of the play into prose but it was composed in long, sonorous alexandrines, painstakingly regular in both rhythm and rhyme.

To read *Gamlet* in the third volume of Sumarokov's *Collected Works*, finely printed by Moscow University Press in 1787, is a rare experience. In comparison with the rude and bawdy *Romeo and Juliet* surviving in the German version discussed above, it strikes one as a highly polished piece of craftsmanship; in fact too polished to convey the immense variety of Shakespeare's dramatic action, imagery, and thought. The influence of French neoclassical drama can be seen not only in the use of alexandrines but also in the strict observance of the unities of time, place, and action, as well as in the conflict between love and duty, passion and reason.

Nothing supernatural like the Ghost is permitted within the Danish royal palace, where the whole action takes place. Instead, Hamlet reveals in his opening soliloquy that he was confronted with his dead father in a frightful dream in which the father, with a wound between his ribs, cried:

> My son! Exact revenge, revenge against the tyrant
> And set the citizens free!

The number of characters is reduced to ten. There is no room for the play-within-the-play of the travelling company, the clownish antics of the gravedigger and his companion, the madness of Ophelia, or for the final fencing match between Hamlet and Laertes.

All important events of the past and present are narrated by the characters, resulting in a static effect like that of Italian opera, fashionable at that time at the tsarist court. Gradually, it transpires that the chief villain is Polonius, who had encouraged and helped Gertrude and Claudius to do away with old King Hamlet and marry each other. Gertrude, however, repents during her first appearance and becomes an ally of her son against her second husband whom she exhorts to repent, too. In a soliloquy fairly close to Shakespeare, Claudius confesses his sins in prayer but is not willing to give up his usurped sceptre. Prodded by Polonius, he decides to pursue the path of power and earthly pleasure. A plot is hatched between Claudius and Polonius to murder both Prince Hamlet and Gertrude and marry off Ophelia to Tsar Claudius.

Ophelia refuses to comply and declares, in a soliloquy of high integrity, her everlasting loyalty to duty and her love for Hamlet to whom she is determined to remain true in all circumstances, whether he becomes the tsar or a slave. In assertion of his patriarchal authority, Polonius condemns Ophelia to death along with Hamlet and Gertrude. His murderous schemes, however, are thwarted when Prince Hamlet, supported by the people, overcomes fifty mercenaries hired by Polonius, kills Claudius, and, entreated by Ophelia, spares Polonius who, nevertheless, commits suicide, cursing both his daughter and Hamlet.

The final speech is given, rather surprisingly, to Ophelia. She is satisfied to have fulfilled her filial duties in defending her father, accepts his death as God's just punishment, and encourages the victorious Hamlet to present himself to the people in the cathedral, where his mother has taken refuge. Her last line is strangely ambiguous:

> And I will go to pay my final debt to nature.

This has usually been interpreted as her willingness to perform the last rites for her dead father but it can also suggest that she herself is ready to die.

In observance of the neoclassical rule of poetic justice, Sumarokov's tragedy ends with the punishment of the usurping tyrant and the triumph of the son of the legitimate ruler. It does not go so far, however, as to announce a wedding between young Hamlet and Ophelia, as some eighteenth-century French and German adaptations did.[1]

One more feature of Sumarokov's *Gamlet* deserves attention. The only soliloquy of Prince Hamlet which is preserved in a recognizable rendering is the central one in Act 3, Scene 1. It is transferred pointedly to the very end of the act and, characteristically for Sumarokov, it does not start with 'To be, or not to be' but with a more concrete question: 'What to do now?' At the close of the soliloquy, Hamlet decides not to commit suicide, giving a definite reason for his decision: his conscience prompts him to help his unhappy country and its oppressed people by punishing the tyrants. The recurrent concern with the fate of the commons may have been invigorated in Sumarokov's mind and imagination by reading Shakespeare. It became one of the central issues of Russian political and literary discourse in the nineteenth century.

Before leaving the eighteenth century, however, we should look at the most surprising adapter of Shakespeare: Tsarina Catherine II, the Great (ruled 1762–96). Although Byron satirized her in *Don Juan* as a 'bold and bloody' empress who was giving most of her 'juicy vigour' to 'love, or lust', she also admired and studied such graver men as Voltaire, Diderot, or Locke and was busy with projects of social reform, until revolts at home and revolutions abroad turned her into an increasingly conservative, autocratic, and imperialist ruler. Nevertheless, she did not cease to support literature and theatre as a means of educating her subjects. Besides a number of treatises, satires, and tales for children, she found time to write fourteen comedies, five comic operas, and three historical plays. German by origin, she was intent on overcoming the one-sided influence of French neoclassicism by reading Shakespeare in German prose translations.

Inspired by them, she concocted a Russified version of *The Merry Wives of Windsor* under the jocular title *This Is What it Means to have a Buck-Basket and Linen* (pub. and acted 1786), introducing it with a disarmingly frank description: 'A free but weak translation from Shakespeare.' This was the first time that Shakespeare's name had appeared on a Russian title-page, as Sumarokov did not mention it anywhere in his adaptation of *Hamlet*. Sumarokov's practice was not unusual for that period when plays were mostly known and performed under their titles; by an amusing, though rather characteristic confusion, a Russian periodical informed its readers in 1731 that Hamlet and Othello were the authors of outstanding comedies.

Catherine's playful title echoed Master Ford's both frantic and comic exclamation at the close of Act 3 of *The Merry Wives*: 'This 'tis to be married! This 'tis to have linen and buck-baskets!' The name of

Windsor did not fit in the Russian title because the whole action was shifted to St Petersburg and most of the characters were given Russified names.

Accordingly, Justice Shallow comes on as Shalov, his foolish cousin Slender as Lyalyukin, the Welsh parson Sir Hugh Evans is turned into the typically Slavonic matchmaker Vanov, Master Page becomes Papin, his wife and daughter receive the Slavonic feminine ending Papina, Master Ford is changed easily into Fordov, his wife into Fordova, etc. Only the French physician Doctor Caius retains his name in a Franco-Russified form Cajou, while his housekeeper Mistress Quickly is reshaped into a French shopkeeper called Madame Quiela who speaks broken Russian infused with French but keeps her basic function of an efficient go-between.[2]

The most daring metamorphosis, however, can be observed in Falstaff. He is called Polkadov and represents a Frenchified Russian dandy who has just returned from expensive travels in Western Europe and shows off in smart clothes, shoes, and hairstyle, all fashioned in the latest Parisian mode, exuding the odour of French perfumes, powder, and tobacco. Turning up his nose at anything Russian, he decks out his speeches with French phrases and expletives, such as 'Chez nous à Paris' or 'Parbleu!' Instead of Falstaff's soft spot for sack (sweet Spanish wine like sherry or canary), he adores French sweet wines and champagne, although the other characters drink homely Russian vodka or English beer. In his desperate search for money and amorous adventure, Polkadov, like Falstaff, falls into the three snares set for him by the merry wives and is repeatedly punished for his lechery, the last time by a whole array of wild men of the woods, witches, and wizards who draw him into a frantic midnight dance and burn him with tapers.

With the substantial changes in the character of Falstaff, Shakespeare's farcical comedy acquired new features of a fairly sharp satire against the aping of Western models and ways of life, so common in St Petersburg high society of that time, and later. In this respect, the Tsarina showed considerable skill in updating Shakespeare's play both politically and linguistically.

Her adaptation is written in straightforward prose, enriched by Russian proverbs and sayings, such as 'money can buy you a village, but a wife is a gift of fate'. The whole structure of *The Merry Wives* is followed pretty faithfully but it is divided into much shorter scenes;

several scenes are cut completely. Paradoxically, in a few instances, Catherine improved on Shakespeare's evidently hasty plotting by leaving out incidents that are not fully resolved in the original, especially the quarrel between Dr Caius, Sir Hugh Evans, and the Host of the Garter Inn. The hilarious Welsh corruption of English by Evans is compensated for by a double French corruption of Russian by both Doctor Cajou and Madame Quiela. Some of the brightest flashes of Shakespeare's humour and poetry are lost or diluted in the adaptation, especially the colossal presence and verbal brilliance of the fat knight, the bombast of Pistol, and the playfully poetic atmosphere of the closing scene.

On the whole, however, Catherine's choice of the *Merry Wives* for her adaptation was clever because the play's prose could be rendered more satisfactorily than the dramatic poetry of the great plays. According to her own statement in her famous correspondence, Catherine never in her life managed to write poetry or music. It is therefore assumed that the few lines of rhymed verse in her adaptation were supplied by her secretary.

The Tsarina liked to be flattered by the saying that while Peter the Great created human beings in Russia, Catherine the Great gave them a soul. Perhaps soul is too great a word for the Tsarina's achievement but it is only fair to say that she enriched Russian culture and civilization with touches of Shakespearian humour and her own sharp wit.

Catherine's creative shortcomings became much more evident in her second Shakespearian adaptation, *The Spendthrift*, based on a German translation of *Timon of Athens*. Her encounter with Shakespeare's most bitter tragedy was certainly courageous but it was destined for failure. With the last act unfinished, *The Spendthrift* was not acted or printed in Catherine's time; only later did it start to be included in her *Collected Works*.

The substantial body of *The Spendthrift*, written in a rather flat prose, allows us to assume that this time Catherine's primary aim was not so much satirical as moral and didactic. She wanted to warn not only against profligate spending but also against the corrupting power of money and gold. As in her previous adaptation, she abandoned Shakespeare's setting, replacing mythical Athens with a street, a house, and a forest presumably in or near St Petersburg, and she converted Timon into Tratov (in Russian, 'Spender'), the revengeful captain Alcibiades into a more conciliatory Bragin, etc. In a moralizing way, she turned Alcibiades' two whores into Bragin's three sisters, the youngest of whom refused to be won by gold and was evidently destined to bring about Tratov's reformation. There can be little doubt that in the end Tratov was to marry her and regain his place in society as a happier and a wiser man.

All this looks like a pale reflection of the original play. Nevertheless, it is remarkable that of all Shakespeare's tragedies the Tsarina was attracted by such a fierce and harsh satire on human nature and society.

Catherine's enchantment with Shakespeare lasted for only about six months of the year 1786. Between writing her two adaptations, she composed, in her usual tearing hurry, two Russian plays, describing them both as 'An imitation of Shakespeare, without observing the usual rules of the theatre'. There was a polemical thrust in this description, aimed at the rigorous rules of the French neoclassical drama and dramatic theory.

The plays were entitled *From the Life of Rurik* and *The Beginning of the Rule of Oleg*, and they were written with the broad sweep and structural freedom of Shakespeare's histories. While Shakespeare sought out his historical material in Holinshed and other English chronicles, Catherine turned to old Russian annals, going much further back to the almost mythical ninth and tenth centuries.

The poetry and richly varied prose of Shakespeare's historical plays was clearly beyond the reach of Catherine, whose own prose was precise but rather cold. Only rarely was she able to capture something of Shakespeare's patriotic fervour in the character of Rurik, who is reminiscent, in his bravery, wisdom, and sense of justice, of the best features of Henry V. The victorious Oleg, standing in full armour with a drawn sword before the walls of Constantinople, also reminds us of Henry V laying siege to Harfleur. Henry's night talk with his three common soldiers before the decisive battle of Agincourt might have stimulated Catherine to introduce three soldiers in the Russian camp near Kiev.

For the most part, however, Catherine's characters appear as wooden mouthpieces for uttering her own moral lessons or retailing historical facts drawn from the annals. Even so, there can be no denying the Tsarina's achievement in, first of all, choosing Shake-speare in preference to the still strongly prevailing French neoclassical models and, secondly, using her paramount influence to inspire Russian theatre with Shakespeare's dramatic, if not poetic, art.

The man of letters who did most for a fuller understanding of Shakespeare in Russia in the eighteenth century was Nikolay Karamzin (1766–1826), best known for his massive unfinished work *A History of the Russian State*, in which he was absorbed during the last decade of his life. As a young man, in 1787, just one year after the Tsarina's Shakespearian adventure, he published *Julius Caesar*, probably the first Russian translation based primarily on Shakespeare's original and introduced by an important preface.

Karamzin was familiar with French prose translations and criticism of Shakespeare, including Voltaire's remarkably faithful rendering of the play, but also with English editors and scholars and with Lessing, the founder of the Shakespeare cult in Germany. Most of all, however, he relied on Shakespeare's original text, translating it, according to his own words, 'faithfully', never changing 'the ideas of my Author'. If he departed from any image of the play, he duly noted it in his detailed commentary. A good example is Act 2, Scene 1, where Brutus gives the motives for the conspirators' opposition to Caesar's tyranny:

> the face of men,
> The sufferance of our souls, the time's abuse – (2.1.113–14)

This is rendered by Karamzin with a sharper political edge as 'the honour of our nation, the deep sense of the breath of freedom, and the pernicious state of our time'. In the footnote, Shakespeare's original is quoted and a literal translation is added to show the extent of the departure.

Brutus' famous speech to the plebeians after the assassination of Caesar (3.2.13–33) is given both in translation and in the original on the same page. Although the whole tragedy is rendered in prose, Shakespeare's transitions from verse into prose and vice versa are recorded in the footnotes. No changes in Shakespeare's setting of scenes or the Roman names of the characters are introduced.

There is a marked difference between the amusing amateurish adaptations of Catherine II, hastily packing Shakespeare's buck-baskets with Russian linen, and the painstaking artistic endeavours of the young Karamzin, who was soon to become a master of Russian prose and leader of the sentimentalist movement asserting a new, natural, and lively style against the artificialities of traditional writers.

In the preface, Karamzin gave firm expression to the dissatisfaction of the Tsarina and a few Russian critics with the rules of the French neoclassical drama and criticism which were still deeply rooted and strongly defended in Russia and elsewhere on the Continent. Taking issue with Voltaire, Karamzin argued that Shakespeare could not observe 'the rules of the theatre' because his ardent imagination could not be bound by any prescriptions:

He did not want to conform to the so-called *unities* which are so rigidly kept by our present dramatic authors; he did not want to impose narrow limits on his imagination; he looked only at Nature and did not care about anything else. He knew that man's mind could fly instantly from the furthest reaches of the Moguls to the bounds of England. His genius, like the genius of Nature, embraced both the sun and the atoms within its vision. He portrayed with equal art a hero and a jester, the wise and the foolish, Brutus and the Cobbler. His plays, like the immense theatre of Nature, are full of variety; but everything is brought together to compose a perfect whole which is in no need of improvement by our present-day *dramatic* authors.[3]

Similar views crop up also in Karamzin's own poetry, prose, and criticism. His popular *Letters of a Russian Traveller* (pub. 1791–2), inspired by Sterne's *Sentimental Journey*, recorded his disappointment with the Haymarket *Hamlet* which he saw during his visit to London in the summer of 1790 (Letter 195). More important was his long reflection on French theatre (Letter 128). Extolling French tragedies for their exquisite imagery and elegant style, he found them more suitable for reading than acting. In a footnote, he challenged the experts on French theatre to offer from Corneille or Racine anything comparable to Lear's agony in the storm. After quoting Lear's lines starting with 'Blow, winds...' (*The Tragedy of King Lear*, 3.2.1–20) both in the original and his own prose translation, he enthused:

They rend the soul; they thunder like the thunder described in them, capturing the reader's heart. What is it that gives them their astonishing power? The extreme situation of the expelled ruler, the living image of his miserable fate. After that there is no need to ask: What is Lear's character, what is his soul?

Karamzin's sensitive insight into *King Lear* was far ahead not only of his own time but also of the times to come, as will become apparent when we discuss Count Lev Tolstoy's attack on Shakespeare, and especially *King Lear*, at the beginning of the twentieth century. Tolstoy's main critical failure was his total neglect of the poetic and dramatic qualities of the tragedy which had been marked out by Karamzin so long ago.

It was also significant that Karamzin chose *Julius Caesar* for his translation and that he considered Brutus the chief hero of the tragedy. The conflict between republican ideals and the harsh realities of absolute political power represented Karamzin's own lifelong dilemma. As late as 1818, when his youthful enthusiasm for 'the breath of freedom' was succeeded by conservative views, he wrote to a friend: 'I shall remain a republican in my heart and, at the same time, a loyal subject of the Russian Tsar.' He must have learned his lesson when his translation of the 'republican tragedy' was burnt with other radical literature in 1794, while the French Revolution was at its height and the frightened Tsarina started to suppress free thought and its exponents.

Copies of Karamzin's *Julius Caesar* with his remarkable preface became very rare in Russia. Fortunately, two of them got into the hands of the most prominent Russian supporters of Shakespeare in the first half of the nineteenth century: the poet Pushkin and the critic Belinsky.

The number of Russian translations, adaptations, and critical discussions of Shakespeare grew steadily in the first decades of the nineteenth century. In the native Russian drama, also, Shakespeare's influence was becoming more and more pronounced. This development reached its climax in Alexander Pushkin (1799–1837), the founder of modern Russian literature, who completed the process of borrowing from Europe and created original works inspired in many ways by his close reading of 'Father Shakespeare', as he lovingly called him.

Although he was born into the ancient landed gentry, with an infusion of African blood from his maternal great-grandfather, an Ethiopian prince who became famous at the court of Peter the Great, Pushkin was exiled from St Petersburg for his youthful anti-despotic verses. He had to live first in the south of Russia, where he composed Byronic poems in 1820–4, and then at his family's estate in the cold north-west. To overcome his feelings of separation from his liberal friends, he started to write a historical tragedy, *Boris Godunov*, his first and best play. In a letter to a friend in 1825, he pondered in French on tragedy 'en général' and, after ridiculing the rigidity of the neoclassical dramatic rules, he exclaimed: 'To create convincing situations and natural dialogues, that's the true rule of a tragedy. I have read neither Calderon nor Vega, but what a man this Shakespeare is. I'm simply bowled over! How petty Byron the tragedian looks if compared with him!' 'Read Shakespeare, that is my refrain,' he insisted, ending his letter in elation: 'I feel that my soul has expanded suddenly, and I can create.'[4]

This creative upsurge can be felt in every scene of the play. Dedicated to the 'dear memory' of Nikolay Karamzin, whose *History of the Russian State*, supplemented by old Russian chronicles, served Pushkin as his source of historical information and inspiration, it dramatized one of the most stirring periods in Russian history: the reign of Boris Godunov (1598–1605) which, by chance, coincided with Shakespeare's most fruitful activity in London. It must have dawned on Pushkin that the tragic beginning of the 'Time of Troubles' in Russia showed many similarities to the dynastic struggles for power between the Lancastrians and the Yorkists covered by Shakespeare in his two cycles of historical plays.

According to Karamzin, Boris secured his position by having Feodor's lawful heir, a boy of 12, secretly murdered. This sinister act enabled the emergence of a Pretender who claimed the crown as the son of Ivan the Terrible, although, in reality, he was a young monk with a temperament too daring for the monastery. Escaping to Poland, he was received with open arms and soon provided with an army and a bride. His invasion of Russia caused a mental upheaval in Boris whose pangs of conscience for the murder of the young Tsarevitch and feelings of frustration at his failure to win popular support were aggravated to such an extent that he ended in mental breakdown and death. The Pretender's way was now open, and he did not scruple to overcome his last obstacle, Boris's son, by having him and his mother mercilessly done away with.

Pushkin dramatized those events in twenty-three scenes covering seven years and shifting freely from crowded Moscow to a secluded monastery in the depth of Russia, a tavern at the Lithuanian border, two palaces in ancient towns of Poland and Galicia, a battlefield in north-west Russia, and back to Moscow for the final tragic catastrophe. The quick changes of scene required corresponding transitions of mood from political tension to comic relief, from the calm serenity of a monastery or a palace garden to the storm and stress of a battlefield or mass gathering.

For this varied and dynamic structure, Pushkin followed Shakespeare, in a radical departure from the traditional drama of the eighteenth and nineteenth centuries. Pushkin's versification also bore Shakespeare's unmistakable signature: *Boris Godunov* is mostly in blank verse with occasional transitions into prose or rhymed lines. The most Shakespearian feature of Pushkin's tragedy, however, is the characterization. Both the title hero and his chief opponent, the False Dimitry, are portrayed with great objectivity, evoking Shakespeare's balancing of Richard II and Bolingbroke in their struggle for power. Boris has much in common with Bolingbroke, ascending and defending the English throne as Henry IV. Both rulers are astute, efficient, and seriously concerned about domestic and foreign affairs but they are also possessed with the desire to preserve the usurped throne for their children. Boris's last speech of advice to his young son bears a strong resemblance to 'the very latest counsel' of King Henry IV to Prince Henry (*2 Henry IV*, 4.3.311–48). At the same time, both Henry IV and Boris realize what a burden it is to wield supreme power, especially when they are supported by courtiers as devious as themselves:

Uneasy lies the head that wears a crown. (*2 Henry IV*, 4.3.31)

How heavy are you, crown of Monarchy! (*Boris Godunov*, end of Scene 10)

In other situations, Boris assumes the brazen attitude of Richard III. Both of them reach power over the corpse of the rightful heir and use similar tactics in accepting the crown: they feign humility and reluctance, seeking refuge in religious contemplation, but finally they comply with the entreaties of the populace. The difference is that Richard shamelessly simulates his religious devotion, whereas Boris is deeply devout to the last moments of his life, taking monastic vows on his deathbed.

Boris's opponent, the False Pretender Dimitry, is not simply a foolhardy adventurer but also an amiable young man, brave and magnanimous. He falls in love with the beautiful and excessively ambitious Polish lady Marina with complete abandon and is ready to give up the whole of Russia for their mutual private happiness. He even goes so far as to tell her about his real origin and only when she threatens to expose him as an impostor does he assume the self-assertive role of Angelo in *Measure for Measure*, rebutting her threats with the power of his social position and reputation. Perhaps the best characterization of the Pretender is given later on in the play by an undaunted Russian prisoner-of-war who tells him to his face that people think him 'a rascal but also a jolly good fellow'.

Not to exaggerate Shakespeare's influence on *Boris Godunov* it is necessary to mention at least two characters in the play who are perfectly original and undoubtedly outstanding. The first is the imposing figure of the old monastic chronicler Pimen who towers above the tempests of confusion and passion like an embodiment of eternal truth. He has the greatness and incorruptible severity of the ancient Chorus, revealing the crimes of the past and pointing to the vanity of ambition and worldly success. Another typically Russian character is introduced by Pushkin's Idiot, Nikolka the Yurodivy, a Fool of Christ, wearing an iron cap and iron chains, and surrounded by a bunch of boys who torment him. He accosts Tsar Boris in front of Moscow Cathedral and asks him to cut the throats of the tormenting boys as he had cut the throat of the boy Tsarevitch. The courtiers try to chase Nikolka away, but Boris orders them to leave him alone and asks him humbly to pray for him. The Idiot's reply is blunt: 'No, no, I cannot pray for King-Herod, the Mother of God does not allow it.' Some critics have argued that the model for Pushkin's Idiot was the Fool in *King Lear*, and the connection between the two characters cannot be ignored. At the same time, the scene shows how creative Pushkin was when inspired by Shakespeare.

Another scene reminiscent of Shakespeare takes place on the battle-field in north-west Russia where Boris's army is retreating before the attack of the Pretender, and two foreign mercenaries, a talkative Frenchman and a dour German, try in vain to stop the fight. Critics have noted some similarities between the two foreign officers in Boris's pay and the Welsh, Irish, and Scottish captains Fluellen, Macmorris, and Jamy in *Henry V*. It seems, however, that Pushkin was more attracted by another soldier of the Agincourt battle: Ancient Pistol, whose encounter with a yielding French nobleman is full of comic linguistic misunderstandings. Remarkably, the retreating Russian soldiers in *Boris Godunov* mock the French captain Margeret, when he does not understand them and asks helplessly, 'Quoi, Quoi?' This reminds them of the croaking of a frog, and so they call him 'an overseas Frog' in the same way the English have popularly derided the French for centuries.

Pushkin and Shakespeare had much in common in their attitude to the common people. They could represent individual figures with unusual vividness or humorous leniency but they realized how fickle and dangerous the people could become when gathered in a multitude and manipulated by ambitious politicians. In *Boris Godunov*, the people first appear in Red Square and immediately afterwards in front of a Moscow monastery in which Boris has taken refuge in religious retreat. In the crowd, Pushkin introduces a woman with a small baby who is crying all the time until the moment comes when everybody is exhorted to cry and implore Boris to accept the crown. Exactly at that moment, the baby stops crying and has to be flung to the ground by its mother to start it screaming again. Two men in the crowd try hard to cry, too, but their eyes remain obstinately dry so that one of them looks for an onion and the other one uses his own saliva to make himself look tearful. At last, Boris accepts the crown, and they all chant: 'Boris is now our Tsar! Long live Boris!'

In the finale of the tragedy, however, a different situation is presented. Although the first draft of the play ended with the compliant people chanting 'Long live Tsar Dimitry!' in approval of the victorious Pretender, Pushkin altered the final version to give it a new, foreboding meaning. When Boris's wife and his son Feodor, who was supposed to succeed him, are murdered by order of the Pretender, the crowd, standing in front of Boris's Kremlin palace, are not ready to accept the concocted news that they had poisoned themselves, since their death cries could be heard by everybody. Instead, according to Pushkin's final stage direction, 'The people, in astonishment, are silent.' When urged to call 'Long live Dimitry Ivanovitch', they still do not reply: 'The people remain silent.'

By contrast with Shakespeare, whose tragedies end with the search for the restoration of order and justice or at least, like *King Lear*, for human composure, Pushkin decided not to attempt an upward turn. Instead, he presented a scene more in keeping with the fate of the long-suffering people of Russia who had to witness the cruelties of their rulers without a chance to oppose them effectively. At best, they could remain silent, or rise in desperate revolts doomed to merciless suppression. All this calls to mind the prophetic words of the Scrivener in *Richard III* (3.6.13–14), expressing the aversion of the common man to the crimes and concealments of the tyrants and the impossibility of speaking openly against them:

> Bad is the world, and all will come to naught,
> When such ill dealing must be seen in thought.

Moreover, in the next scene of *Richard III* (3.7) there is a parallel to Pushkin's tragic catastrophe. The citizens of London 'are mum, say not a word' when expected to accept Richard for their king and, after a long persuading speech by the Duke of Buckingham, they still stand 'like dumb statuas or breathing stones', staring at each other and looking 'deadly pale'.

Immediately after having finished *Boris Godunov*, Pushkin, according to his own words, paced up and down in his room, clapping his hands and crying enthusiastically: 'Well done, Pushkin, that's the stuff, you son of a bitch!' The new Tsar Nicholas I (ruled 1825–55), however, was of a different opinion. Assuming the role of Pushkin's benevolent personal censor, he advised him to rewrite the play, leaving out offending passages, into a novel in the manner of Sir Walter Scott! Such a ridiculous piece of advice could not be taken seriously, so the play had to wait for its first edition, shortened by cuts, until January 1831 and for its first performance, still in a censored version, until as late as 1870.

Nicholas I's censorship of Pushkin's play was the stricter in that it coincided with the suppression of an uprising of several groups of Russian nobility against tsarist absolutism. The revolt started in December 1825 and its unsuccessful leaders, called the Decembrists, were immediately hanged or sent into exile in Siberia. Pushkin was in broad sympathy with their aims but could see the weakness and isolation of their position. In this critical situation, Shakespeare proved more than a source of artistic inspiration. In a personal letter of January 1826, Pushkin wrote: 'I am impatiently awaiting the announcement of the sentence of the unhappy men. I'm deeply convinced of the magnanimity of the young Tsar. Let us not be superstitious and one-sided like the French tragedians, rather let us look at the tragedy with the eyes of Shakespeare.' Unfortunately, Tsar Nicholas, unlike his grandmother Catherine, showed little understanding of Shakespeare and his great Russian disciple.

About the same time, still in the solitude of his family estate, Pushkin read *The Rape of Lucrece*, 'a rather weak poem by Shakespeare', as he brusquely called it. Suddenly, he wondered what would have happened if the harassed Roman lady had thought of cooling the sexual ardour of her ravisher Tarquin by slapping his face. The whole course of early Roman history would have been changed! Lucrece would not have been raped and would not have committed suicide, and the Romans would not have expelled the tyrannical Tarquins to constitute a republic.

On the spur of sudden inspiration Pushkin composed a short narrative poem, *Count Nulin* (pub. 1828), a mock-heroic parody of Roman history and Shakespeare's early work. He completely abandoned Shakespeare's historical setting because a recent parallel to the central conflict, in his own neighbourhood, flashed across his mind. His burlesque became a mildly satirical picture of Russian provincial life in which a God-forsaken village is visited by the title hero whose allegorical name suggests a great disparity between his aristocratic title and his personal worth (Nulin = Zero, Nobody). As a Frenchified Russian fop, Count Nulin bears a strong resemblance to Polkadov-Falstaff, the comic seducer in Catherine II's adaptation of *The Merry Wives*. Otherwise, however, there is no comparison between the Tsarina's flat prose adaptation of Shakespeare's comedy and Pushkin's sparkling parody of Shakespeare's poem. Although *Count Nulin* was dashed off with extraordinary ease in two successive mornings, it played an important part in Pushkin's artistic development because it absorbed incidental motifs and allowed him to concentrate on his greatest work, the novel in verse *Eugene Onegin* (1823–31).

In 1830 Pushkin wrote four short plays called by later critics *Little Tragedies*. At least two of them bear unmistakable traces of Shakespeare's influence. In *The Stone Guest* the blank verse rendering of the highly popular theme of Don Juan leads to a striking ending in which both the dark hero and Donna Anna are damned by the stone statue of Anna's murdered husband. The central encounter between Don Juan and Donna Anna shows a remarkable similarity to the daredevil wooing of Lady Anne by Richard III (*Richard III*, 1.2.34–214). Both wooers go so far as to offer their bared breasts for the mourning ladies to kill them—or to love them. This brazen courage completely confuses both women.

In *The Covetous Knight* Pushkin's blank verse reached maturity marked by frequent feminine endings and run-on lines. The critic Belinsky expressed his admiration of this dramatic miniature set in the late Middle Ages: 'In its well-sustained characters (the miser, his son, the Duke, and the Jew), its skilful arrangement, and its ending,—in short, in everything—, this drama is a great achievement, worthy of the genius of Shakespeare himself.'

Pushkin was deeply impressed by the complexity of Shakespeare's characters, especially Shylock, Angelo, and, most of all, Falstaff. Strangely enough, neither Hamlet nor Lear attracted his special attention.

After his marriage, in 1831, to a famous young beauty, Natalia Goncharova, whose honour he would later defend in a fatal duel of 1837, Pushkin intensified his literary activities in search of badly needed income. In 1833, he started, among other projects, to translate Shakespeare's *Measure for Measure*, but his creative urge for independence forced him to give up translating and to turn the plot of Shakespeare's dark comedy into a verse tale in alexandrine stanzas of varying length. Calling it *Angelo*, he shifted the place of action from Vienna to Italy, left out all the minor characters and the whole comic sub-plot, reduced the Duke's role to the opening and the closing of the action, and concentrated on the conflict between the hypocritical machiavellian governor Angelo and the inflexibly devout nun Isabella. Their dialogues are rendered with great vividness and dramatic tension.

Pushkin's indebtedness to Shakespeare was strong and lasting, surpassing his youthful enthusiasm for Byron. At the same time, although he was called both 'Russian Byron' and 'Russian Shakespeare', he was an original poet who carried the literature of his country to its first summit, linking Russian culture with the cultural heritage and inspiration of Western Europe, especially Britain. By the irony of fate, the verse of this most gifted literary craftsman was for a long time at the mercy of inferior English and American translators. In addition, Pushkin's poetry, like most Slavonic poetry, yields very grudgingly to being rendered into foreign languages. Consequently, as late as 1887 Matthew Arnold, in his essay on Tolstoy, passed a characteristic though unfounded judgement: 'The crown of literature is poetry, and the Russians have not yet had a great poet.' Even today, although the considerable number of Pushkin's translators has been increased by

Maurice Baring, D. M. Thomas, Vladimir Nabokov, and Sir Charles Johnston, Pushkin remains abroad probably the least read of all the major Russian authors. At home, however, he has been among the most beloved.

Pushkin's untimely death was lamented by the most characteristic representative of Russian Romanticism, Mikhail Lermontov (1814–41). His indignant, fiery poem 'The Death of a Poet' (1837) brought him immediate fame but also punitive service in the Caucasus. Lermontov shared with Pushkin several basic affinities: aristocratic background with a foreign ancestor (he descended from a Scottish officer, Captain George Learmont, who entered tsarist service in the early seventeenth century); fascination with Byron and lasting admiration for Shakespeare; original contributions not only to poetry but also to verse drama and prose; and premature death in a duel.

Russian and Estonian scholars have spotted echoes of Shakespeare in both Lermontov's poetry and his drama. The most conspicuous Shakespearian inspiration can be seen in *The Masquerade* (1836, first printed 1842, first produced 1862), a poetic tragedy of jealousy, in which the central motif of the lost and manipulated bracelet of the tragic heroine Nina clearly recalls Desdemona's lost and misused handkerchief. Desdemona's 'Willow Song' may have prompted Nina's highly romantic song in Act 3, Scene 1. In the desperate defence of their virtue and their young lives Nina and Desdemona have much in common. The tragic hero Arbenin succumbs to jealousy with the same blind reliance on ocular proof as Othello, and assumes a similar role as supreme judge of his wife's surmised adultery. When he kisses her just after poisoning her, he brings to mind Othello kissing Desdemona before killing her and then dying upon another kiss. There is a general resemblance between Arbenin and the proud, demonic, and world-weary heroes of Byron with their mysterious suffering, loves, and hatreds. Some of Arbenin's features, however, point to Hamlet whose 'noble mind' seems to Ophelia to be 'o'erthrown'. Arbenin's 'proud mind' breaks down completely in the end. Paradoxically, his chief rival considers him, in the last speech of the tragedy, 'happy' in his madness.

Although Lermontov departed from Shakespeare and Pushkin, and also from Byron's blank verse dramas, by using the more traditional rhymed verse, he achieved a surprising fluency of both dialogues and monologues and a truly Byronic elegance, ironic wit, and satirical incisiveness. The free Shakespearian dramatic structure enabled him to move the action smoothly from a gambling house to aristocratic palaces, where intimate scenes are contrasted with a masquerade and a ball of high Petersburg society, presented in all its outward splendour and inward hollowness filled with petty, malicious gossip which poisons both friendship and love.

II

Turning to criticism, the first major and very influential critic in Russia, Vissarion Belinsky (1811–48), retained, until his premature death, an unreserved enthusiasm for Shakespeare, whom he ranked above the dramatists of ancient Greece as well as the neoclassical French and the recent German drama. Shakespeare was for him 'the king of nature' who presented life with supreme impartiality and embraced not only earth but also heaven and hell.

Belinsky's essay on *Hamlet* (1838), unusually long and discursive, owes a good deal to German philosophy, especially to Hegel and his followers, and also to Goethe's views on Shakespeare and *Hamlet* in particular. It elucidates Hamlet as a dramatic character who is undergoing a process of total disintegration of his noble ideals but finally reaches the recognition that 'The readiness is all.' This idea of Hamlet's spiritual progress is evidently based on the Hegelian dialectical triad of thesis (youthful idealism)–antithesis (disintegration)–synthesis (recognition or discovery of truth).

Belinsky's discussion of *Hamlet* was closely connected with the interpretation of the title role by the Russian romantic actor Pavel Mochalov at the Moscow Small (Maly) Theatre in 1837. Belinsky was present at eight of Mochalov's performances and was so impressed that he devoted half of his essay to him. In this way, Belinsky's essay became a very early precursor of what is called today performance criticism.

Belinsky described the Moscow production scene by scene, concentrating on Mochalov's acting, pointing out both his weak and strong moments. He showed how Mochalov was able to overcome the disadvantage of his small figure and rather thin voice, which restricted his delivery of the soliloquies, by the expressiveness of his handsome pale face and piercing eyes. In most scenes, Mochalov hypnotized his audiences into an unforgettable experience of watching a great soul shattered by infinite pain and sorrow but resisting his despair by pursuing his inescapable task: to expose and punish the usurping king.

It is evident that Mochalov gave his Hamlet much more energy and strength of will than could be derived directly from the rather smooth Russian translation of Shakespeare's text. His volcanic outbursts reflected the spirit of resistance and civil disobedience which was rising again among the Russian intelligentsia after the suppression of the Decembrist insurrection, as the growth of radically democratic ideas and movements led to the revolutions in Poland, Bohemia, Austria, Hungary, and other European countries in 1830–1 and 1848–9. We can understand that it was impossible for Belinsky to express his democratic ideas directly in the face of the strict tsarist censorship. But it was possible for Mochalov and his critic to show that the sorrows of young Hamlet could be turned into 'rancorous indignation' and 'feverish fury', as Belinsky put it.

Although the number of Russian translations of Shakespeare was growing apace, not all were allowed to be performed. There are records of the suppression of productions of *Henry IV* (1840), *Julius Caesar* (1845), *Richard III* (1851), and even of *The Comedy of Errors* (1840) and *Cymbeline* (1853). *Macbeth* was approved for performance, with considerable cuts, only in 1860. A whole group of official Petersburg critics was mobilized to launch a campaign against Shakespeare, whose plays came to be considered by the authorities as incendiary.

Nevertheless, Mochalov's Hamlet was brought to the Russian mind again by Ivan Turgenev (1818–83), who could not easily be suppressed because he was the first novelist to win full recognition for Russian literature in the West, where he lived for long periods of his life. As a young man, Turgenev saw Mochalov play Hamlet in Moscow and did not hesitate to recall him later as 'the great Russian, very Russian actor'.

After a longer stay in Western Europe, Turgenev returned to Russia in 1850 but in 1852 he was arrested by the tsarist police and held in rural isolation for a year and a half. One of the main reasons for the exile was his literary and civic support for the emancipation of the serfs. Undaunted, he continued in his efforts until Tsar Alexander II (ruled 1858–81) abolished serfdom in 1861.

Following Belinsky, Turgenev admired Shakespeare immensely, comparing him to Nature, 'simple yet infinitely varied, harmonious, wise and free'. In his tales, novels, and essays, Turgenev developed the view that two basic types prevailed in mankind generally and among the Russian intelligentsia in particular: Hamlets and Don Quixotes. In a thought-provoking paper read and published in 1860 under the title 'Hamlet and Don Quixote: The Two Eternal Human Types', he explained that Don Quixote represented 'Faith, in the first place, faith in something eternal, immutable; faith in the truth, in short, existing *outside* of the individual.'

By contrast, Hamlet represented for Turgenev

Analysis, first of all, and egotism, and therefore lack of faith . . . He is a sceptic and always pothers about himself; he is ever busy, not with his duty, but with his condition. Doubting everything, Hamlet, of course, spares not himself; his mind is too much developed to be satisfied with what he finds within himself. He is conscious of his weakness; but even his self-consciousness is power; from it comes his irony, in contrast with the enthusiasm of Don Quixote. . . . Hamlet embodies the doctrine of negation, that same doctrine which another great poet has divested of everything human and presented in the form of Mephistopheles. Hamlet is the same Mephistopheles, but a Mephistopheles embraced by the living circle of human nature: hence his negation is not an evil, but is itself directed against evil.[5]

It is obvious that Turgenev's interpretation of the character of Hamlet differed substantially from that of Mochalov and Belinsky. It was an early anti-Romantic reading, encouraged by some German critics and preceding by several decades Stéphane Mallarmé, who has usually been considered the pathfinder in stressing the dark aspects of Hamlet's character and thus anticipating G. Wilson Knight, L. C. Knights, Salvador de Madariaga, and similarly oriented critics of the twentieth century.

Turgenev, however, never went so far as to see Hamlet as an egocentric figure of death and evil because he found that 'Hamlet wages relentless war' upon evil. Similarly, Hamlet's scepticism, in Turgenev's reading, 'is irreconcilably at war with falsehood, and through this very quality he becomes one of the foremost champions of a truth in which he himself cannot fully believe'.

Turgenev associated Hamlet with a number of heroes of his own tales and novels, notably his early tale *Hamlet of Shchigrovo* (1849) and his mature novels *Fathers and Sons* (1862), dedicated to the memory of Belinsky, and *Virgin Soil* (1877). He held the highest opinion not only of *Hamlet* but also of *King Lear*, which inspired one of his most mature and forceful tales, *A King Lear of the Steppes* (1870). It is a story of a widowed Russian landlord, a bear-like descendant of an ancient but decrepit family, who takes revenge on his two hard-hearted daughters and his villainous son-in-law by pulling the roof-tree of the house, which he had ceded to them, down on himself. Characteristically, for Turgenev's cosmopolitan orientation, the story combines motifs from *King Lear* with the ending of Milton's *Samson Agonistes*, and ultimately with Samson's fate in the Old Testament.

Many other outstanding Russian writers of the second half of the nineteenth century discussed Shakespeare appreciatively or were inspired by him. For Fyodor Dostoevsky (1821–81), who, as a novelist, emulated Dickens and Walter Scott in the first place, Shakespeare was 'a great prophet sent by God in order to reveal to us the secret of man, of man's soul'.[6] This is what Dostoevsky himself tried to do, and it is not surprising to find numerous Shakespearian echoes, quotations, allusions, and paraphrases in his work. In another statement, he called Shakespeare 'the poet of despair' and, again, this characterization can be applied more appropriately to him and to his unceasing penetration into the irrationality, arbitrariness, and latent destructiveness and self-destructiveness of human nature.

The most attractive play for Dostoevsky was *Hamlet*: its tragic hero expressed for him the heights and depths of self-analysis, mental anguish, and noble suffering. Dostoevsky's notebooks show that he was preoccupied with Shakespeare at the time he was writing his most polemical novel *Devils* (also known as *The Possessed*, 1872), intent on a sweeping refusal of revolutionary materialism and on an apotheosis of orthodox Russian faith. The most enigmatic figure of the novel, Stavrogin, is introduced as 'prince Henry', in a direct reference to Shakespeare's young hero of *Henry IV*. Stavrogin's youthful debauchery in the underworld of St Petersburg is likened to Henry's adventures with Falstaff, Poins, and Mistress Quickly. Although Stavrogin displays distinct features of nihilism, in his mother's eyes he assumes the nobility of Prince Hamlet and lacks only the friendship and the humility of a Horatio to be saved from his melancholy and the demon of scepticism leading him to suicide.

The denunciation of revolutionary nihilism in Stavrogin and other characters was rooted in Dostoevsky's own experience. As a young man he joined a socialist circle which was exposed by the secret police and its members sent, after a macabre mock execution, to a Siberian penal colony. During his four-year imprisonment, followed by another four years of service as a private soldier, Dostoevsky underwent religious conversion, rejected socialism, and embraced the Russian Orthodox Church and the belief in a special mission of the Russian people. Shakespeare was all the more important for him as a counterbalance to his mystical and messianic visions of light coming only from the East.

Further Shakespearian allusions are scattered over Dostoevsky's last and most complex work *The Brothers Karamazov* (1879–80). The eldest brother, Dmitri, a passionate man given to fits of melancholy and despair, associates himself with Hamlet by a curious paraphrase followed by his even more curious identification with Yorick: 'Do you remember *Hamlet*: "I am so sad, so sad, Horatio... Akh, poor Yorick!"... Perhaps I am that Yorick. Just now I'm Yorick, but later a skull.' Dmitri seems to be alluding both to his role as a jester and to his meditated, but not committed, suicide. Suicidal inclinations are realized by Dmitri's alleged stepbrother Smerdyakov after he has killed their father, old Karamazov. At the trial, the Prosecutor reflects: 'Look, gentlemen, look how our young people are shooting themselves: oh, without any trace of Hamletic questions about "What will be there?", without recognition of these questions.' For Dostoevsky the Hamlet question was connected with both the propensity for suicide and the concern about what dreams may come after death. As a whole, echoes of *Hamlet* and weaker traces of *Othello* in *The Brothers Karamazov* contribute to the European resonance and polyphony of views and visions in Dostoevsky's grandiose, unfinished novel.

Impulses from Turgenev's essay on Hamlet and Don Quixote resound creatively through *Ivanov* (1887), the first full-length play by Anton Chekhov (1860–1904). Not only are there direct or paraphrased allusions to Hamlet, Ophelia, and Don Quixote in the text of the play but the title hero has much in common with Turgenev's interpretation of Hamlet's character. He appears as a striking example of the 'superfluous man' of Russian life and literature in the second half of the nineteenth century when the emancipation of the serfs did not stir the expected initiative among them, while radical movements among the intelligentsia were stifled and then crushed after the assassination of Tsar Alexander II in 1881. Although Ivanov, an impoverished country gentleman, is only in his early thirties, he is tired of the burden of life, suffering from melancholy, feeling useless, weary, and wasted. His wife, a young Jewish woman whom he had persuaded to leave her parents and her religion, is dying of tuberculosis after five years of marriage, and he is incapable of giving her consolation by showing his sympathy for her. When the young daughter of his rich neighbour declares her love to him and her readiness to make him happy, he responds enthusiastically for a moment but finally, after his wife's death, decides not to ruin another woman by a new marriage and shoots himself just before the wedding ceremony. His suicide, only contemplated by Hamlet, precipitates the tragic catastrophe.

It is revealing to compare Ivanov's one and only soliloquy (Act 3, Scene 6) with the first three soliloquies of Hamlet (Act 1, Scene 2; Act 2, Scene 2; Act 3, Scene 1). Like Hamlet, Ivanov is nauseated by himself and his weakness, recalling that only a year ago he was strong, courageous, full of energy and fire, stirred by evil, moved by the suffering of others, able to move the very stones to tears. Now his estate is running to waste, his whole country looks forlorn, and all he feels is anxiety and disgust. He accuses himself because, having promised his wife to love her and make her happy, now, when she has fallen ill, he runs away like a coward from her pale face, sunken breast, and beseeching look. The only action he feels ready for is to fire a bullet through his head.

The chief difference between Hamlet and Ivanov is that the latter blames only himself, without accusing the 'slings and arrows of outrageous fortune', 'the whips and scorns of time', or the 'oppressor's wrong'. Neither does he dread the 'undiscovered country' after death. He only feels anguish and fear of the future in which he once believed so enthusiastically. Finally, he refuses to find escape and excuse in the role of the superfluous man and draws uncompromising consequences from his loss of faith and perspective.

Although Ivanov considers only himself to be responsible for his total disintegration, the whole play shows objectively in what an empty, shallow, and disgusting world he has to live. Russian provincial life is represented in all its alcoholic stupor, its addiction to gambling, the incompetence of the degenerate and impoverished aristocracy, the greediness of the *nouveaux riches*, and the laziness of the bureaucrats. There are no prospects opening before the young generation, there is nobody to respond to Ivanov's 'dying voice'.

Chekhov was evidently fascinated with *Hamlet*, and different reflections of the tragedy in his other plays—*The Seagull* (1895), *Uncle Vanya* (1900), or *The Cherry Orchard* (1904)—have been observed. In the last-mentioned sad comedy, there is parodic word-play on the name of Ophelia, when the rich merchant Lopakhin, who is supposed to marry the impecunious young lady Varya but never summons up the courage to do so, calls her Okhmelia and sends her to a nunnery. His blunt joke involves a pun on *khmel* (intoxication, fuddle), suggesting that she is a nymph attracted not by water alone.

The most important affinities between Chekhov and Shakespeare can be seen in their highly objective representation of life, their daring fusion of tragedy, comedy, irony, and satire in one organic whole, and their complex and ambiguous characterization, rich in contradictions, paradoxes, waverings, and incertitudes, allowing for an endless succession of varied interpretations.

Shakespeare's objectivity was branded as 'immoral' in the most provocative Russian essay on Shakespeare, written by Count Lev Tolstoy (1828–1910). Although his friends tried hard to win him over to Shakespeare, Tolstoy remained adamant in his dislike of him, expressed in both private talks and written statements. Naturally, he reproached Chekhov for writing even more badly than Shakespeare.

In 1906 Tolstoy's lengthy study 'On Shakespeare and the Drama' was published simultaneously in Russian in Moscow and in English in London and New York. Even if we take into consideration that it was written during the last, zealously religious phase of Tolstoy's life, there is no reason to doubt his honesty in stressing that his disagreement with the traditional opinion about Shakespeare 'is not the result of an accidental frame of mind nor of a light-minded attitude toward the matter, but the outcome of many years' repeated and insistent endeavors to harmonize my own views of Shakespeare with those established amongst all civilized men of the Christian world'.[7] Stating that he had read Shakespeare's tragedies, comedies, and historical plays repeatedly not only in Russian but also in English and German, he declared bluntly that he 'invariably underwent the same feelings:

repulsion, weariness, and bewilderment'. Even before his final attack he spoke out against Shakespeare many times, evidently exasperated by the verbose and, as he called it, 'epidemic' eulogies of many Western, especially German, critics in the nineteenth century.

His final criticism was meant to be thorough and detailed, prepared by a fresh rereading of Shakespeare's plays and also by the study of Shakespeare's sources and of English, French, Danish, and German Shakespearian criticism. He decided to choose for his close analysis 'one of Shakespeare's most extolled dramas, *King Lear*', and started by quoting appreciative critical opinions of the play by Dr Johnson, Hazlitt, Hallam, Shelley, Swinburne, Hugo, and Brandes. Then he proceeded to describe the action of the tragedy scene by scene 'as impartially as possible' but he could not help dropping in acid remarks about the improbability, absurdity, and confusion of both the plot and the sub-plot as well as about the pretentious and unnatural language and unmotivated behaviour of the main characters. In particular, he complained about Lear's bombastic speeches and the Fool's nonsense and bawdry, which evoked in him the 'wearisome uneasiness which one experiences when listening to jokes which are not witty'. In short, Tolstoy was not amused.

On the contrary, he was offended by what he felt was the play's lack of moral seriousness and artistic merit. He even did not hesitate to declare that the anonymous old play *King Leir*, Shakespeare's main dramatic source, was superior to Shakespeare's tragedy because it did not have the 'utterly superfluous' sub-plot and 'the completely false effects of Lear running about the heath, his conversations with the fool, and all these impossible disguises, failures to recognize, and accumulated deaths'. He concluded his comparison by affirming that in the old drama 'there is the simple, natural and deeply touching character of Leir and the yet more touching and clearly defined character of Cordelia' and that 'instead of Shakespeare's long drawn-out scene of Lear's interview with Cordelia and of Cordelia's unnecessary murder' there is 'the exquisite scene of the interview between Leir and Cordelia, unequalled by any in all of Shakespeare's dramas'.

Extending his critical approach to other plays and characters, Tolstoy approved of Falstaff as 'perhaps the only natural and typical character depicted by Shakespeare'. The more devastating was his criticism of Hamlet:

But in none of Shakespeare's figures is his—I will not say incapacity to give, but utter indifference to giving—his personages a typical character, so strikingly manifest as in *Hamlet*. In connection with none of Shakespeare's works do we see so strikingly displayed that blind worship of Shakespeare, that unreasoning state of hypnotism owing to which even the mere thought is not admitted that any of Shakespeare's productions can be wanting in genius or that any of the principal personages in his dramas can fail to be the expression of a new and deeply conceived character.

Tolstoy regarded all this adoration as a great evil which must be combated. The fundamental cause of Shakespeare's fame was seen by Tolstoy in the fact that his plays 'corresponded to the irreligious and immoral frame of mind of the upper classes of his time and ours'. Therefore he thought it imperative that people of the twentieth century should free themselves of the false and hypnotic glorification of 'the trivial and immoral works of Shakespeare and his imitators'.

Tolstoy's views had some repercussions in the West. Predictably enough, they attracted the attention of G. B. Shaw, another eloquent iconoclast and anti-Romantic critic of Shakespeare's 'romantic nonsense' and of the 'bardolatry' of his worshippers. The ensuing correspondence between the two writers shows, however, that Tolstoy's rejection of Shakespeare was too sweeping even for Shaw, who found many deficiencies in Shakespeare's philosophic and moral views but never ceased to admire his 'enormous command of word music which gives fascination to his most blackguardly repartees and sublimity to his hollowest platitudes'.[8]

Among the infrequent later English reactions to Tolstoy's devastating criticism probably the most remarkable was George Orwell's essay 'Lear, Tolstoy and the Fool' (1947). Choosing an essentially psychoanalytical approach, Orwell formed the hypothesis that the reasons for Tolstoy's hostility were different, or partly different, from what he himself avowed: the basic reason was Tolstoy's subconscious identification of his own fate with that of Lear. Like Lear, Tolstoy in his old age renounced his social position, title, power, and wealth to find that ultimately two of his children turned against him so that he died on a feverish pilgrimage accompanied only by one daughter who remained faithful to him. This would mean that when writing his essay Tolstoy felt Lear's renunciation as an anticipation of his own premeditated abdication, disappointment, passionate denunciation of social injustice, and final tragedy. An additional reason was, according to Orwell, that Tolstoy came to think of Shakespeare's work as something dangerous to himself: the more pleasure people took in Shakespeare, the less would they appreciate Tolstoy and listen to his religious and social teaching. In his pacifism, Tolstoy was also disturbed by Shakespeare's patriotism which sometimes reached the extremes of jingoism, as Shaw called it.

Thought-provoking as Orwell's views were, the chief reason for Tolstoy's rejection of Shakespeare should probably be looked for elsewhere: in the very different world outlooks and artistic methods of the two authors. Shakespeare's prevailing secular humanism must have come more and more into conflict with Tolstoy's growing religious zeal. Moreover, Tolstoy, primarily a novelist, applied his own artistic principles to Shakespeare's poetic dramas, ignoring both their poetic and dramatic quality. While Shakespeare developed the traditions of native English drama, with all its conventions readily accepted by his audiences, Tolstoy, a Russian aristocrat, was steeped in French culture, including the neoclassical ideals of order, naturalness, regularity, preciseness, clarity, verisimilitude, and decorum. Tolstoy seems to have been completely blind and deaf to the richness of Shakespeare's word-play and offended by his daring bawdiness. In short, Tolstoy as a realistic novelist rejected Shakespeare's Renaissance exuberance in plot, language, imagery, and characterization as well as the Romantic enthusiasm for Shakespeare's genius.

In spite of Tolstoy's attack, Shakespeare continued to be read and played all over Russia with undiminished devotion because, according to Turgenev, he had got into Russian 'flesh and blood'. Tolstoy only provoked generations of Russian actors, directors, and critics to define their attitudes towards Shakespeare more consciously and thoroughly.

Between 1902 and 1904 an impressive Russian edition of Shakespeare's *Complete Works* in five illustrated volumes was published in St Petersburg as the culmination of many preceding translations of individual, selected, and collected works in prose or verse. The first edition of selected plays in prose translation appeared between 1841 and 1850; collected plays in verse and prose were first published between 1865 and 1868.

III

In the theatres, a number of Russian actors and actresses excelled in Shakespeare's tragic and comic parts; moreover, foreign stars, such as Ira Aldridge, Ernesto Rossi, or Tommaso Salvini, were invited to play Shakespeare in St Petersburg and Moscow. Ironically, the Afro-American tragedian Aldridge, having no chance of appearing on the American stage, was applauded in the roles of Othello, Macbeth, King Lear, and Richard III both in England and on the Continent, including Eastern and East Central Europe. He died in the Polish town Łódź in 1867.

A new style of ensemble acting, opposed to the supremacy of individual stars, was brought to Russia from Germany in 1885 by the visiting Meiningen Players, founded and directed by the Duke of Saxe-Meiningen. Their opening performance of *Julius Caesar* in St Petersburg was very significant, as it presented a tragedy which had been discovered and interpreted for Russia long ago by Karamzin but was banned from Russian stages because of Brutus' republicanism and his decisive part in the assassination of the dictator. When Alexander II was assassinated in 1881, tsarist authorities became even more watchful, but they did not dare to offend such a noble guest as the German Duke, so that the ban on *Julius Caesar* was partly, if not entirely, lifted. This situation enabled Russian theatres to press for a complete revocation of the ban, and after a less important production in 1897 *Julius Caesar* was produced in 1903 by the most trailblazing Russian company of the time, the Moscow Art Theatre (MAT).

The MAT was founded in 1898 by two artists who were to exercise an unusual influence on the development of Russian and world theatre of the twentieth century: K. S. Stanislavsky and Vladimir Nemirovich-Danchenko. They both won early recognition for the MAT with their pioneering productions of Chekhov, in whose delicate balance of tragedy and comedy they discovered one of the heralds of twentieth-century drama. In their production of *Julius Caesar*, they developed the ensemble playing of the Meiningen Company into a powerful representation of the Roman people forming a huge crowd governed by mass psychology as threatening and unfathomable as the heaving sea. According to the reminiscences of Nemirovich-Danchenko, the central scenes for him and Stanislavsky were the streets of Rome, the senate with the assassination of Caesar, Caesar's funeral, the people's revolt, and the final battles. More than 200 supernumeraries were employed. The principal aim of the directors was to represent Rome in the epoch of Julius Caesar.[9] For better or worse, the production announced a new era of Russian theatre by reflecting the drives of the broad social forces which were suppressed in the immediate revolution of 1905 but signalled the huge outburst in 1917.

The next memorable Shakespearian event at the Moscow Art Theatre took place in 1911–12 when the British director, designer, and theorist Edward Gordon Craig was invited to co-direct *Hamlet* with Stanislavsky. Given the radical difference in the approaches of the two artists to Shakespeare, their production was destined to bring out much more conflict and contrast than smooth cooperation. Craig stressed the mystic symbolism of the tragedy, conceiving it as a dream of the supersensitive Prince who is alienated both from the evil court and from action. Stanislavsky demanded from Hamlet and the other actors his own style of Chekhovian poetic realism, rich in atmospheric and psychological suggestion based on inner experience. Hamlet was played by V. I. Kachalov, who was soft-spoken, melancholy, and fatalistic but not devoid of the capacity for pursuing and purging evil. Although he was a far, soft cry from the volcanic and indignant Mochalov in the Romantic era, he was not as sceptical and neurotic as some 'sick' Russian Hamlets of the first decade of the new century. In a typically Russian way, his suffering and sorrow were for all mankind.

Craig's sets ensured a fluid action by introducing high vertical screens which were easily rearranged into different Cubist patterns according to the changes of scene from battlement to court, bedroom, or graveyard. The final scene showed Hamlet dreaming, in the approach of death, the arrival of Fortinbras with his soldiers who filled the stage, lowering their white banners on the dead body and happy face 'of the great cleanser of the earth who had at last found the secrets of life on earth in the arms of death'.[10]

A balanced evaluation of the MAT *Hamlet* has been proposed by Dennis Kennedy: 'In general terms the performance was either a flawed success or a brilliant failure, depending on the point of view.' In any case, it turned the attention of the West to one of the most avant-garde theatres in the East. It remained in the MAT repertoire for a long time and was performed on a prolonged tour of the company through Europe and America during the Civil War in Soviet Russia. When the company visited Prague in 1921, Kachalov's Hamlet was acclaimed by the leading Czech theatre critic as a noble, rational, and finally happy hero whose mellifluous voice was in harmony with his character. Back at home, Kachalov continued to play the title role until 1940, when he reached the age of 65. The resilience of the MAT company was instrumental in building cultural bridges between tsarist and Bolshevik Russia.

FURTHER READING

For a general survey see Ernest J. Simmons, *English Literature and Culture in Russia 1553–1840* (Cambridge, Mass., 1935). Sumarokov's *Gamlet* is now available in English in *Selected Tragedies of A. P. Sumarokov*, trans. Richard and Raymond Fortune, introd. John Fizer (Evanston, Ill., 1970). Ivan Turgenev's little classic in comparative literature 'Hamlet and Don Quixote: The Two Eternal Human Types' can be read in English translation in Oswald LeWinter (ed.), *Shakespeare in Europe* (Cleveland, 1963; Harmondsworth, 1970). Lev Tolstoy's attack on Shakespeare is also included in LeWinter's volume. Two specialized studies are worth reading: George Gibian, *Tolstoj* [sic] *and Shakespeare* (The Hague, 1957), a well-researched and balanced enquiry into an intriguing problem, and a more substantial monograph by Eleanor Rowe, *Hamlet: A Window on Russia* (New York, 1976).

3

Shakespeare and National Revivals

This chapter takes us back to the mid-eighteenth century when remarkable movements in continental cultural and political life began, continuing well into the nineteenth century, with most momentous repercussions reaching into our own days. It all started in Germany where the middle classes, despite their religious, political, and economic fragmentation into numerous smaller and larger states, felt strong enough to assert their own culture, differentiating themselves from the aristocratic courts steeped in French tradition. As far as theatres were concerned, the dichotomy between court theatres, which tended to preserve the neoclassical hegemony of French tragedy and comedy, and the German strolling companies with their freewheeling repertoires inherited from the English Comedians, was beginning to dissolve. Instead, the increasingly well-to-do middle classes aspired to found national theatres that would appeal to the whole of society while preserving the old aristocratic refinement and decorum. The low-comic figure of Hanswurst, the successor of Pickleherring, was symbolically expelled from the stage by being burnt in effigy.

The first German National Theatre was opened in Hamburg in 1767 and, though lasting a mere two years, prepared the ground for the permanent theatre established there in 1776 by the actor, manager, and Shakespearian adapter F. L. Schröder. Sometimes, enlightened rulers themselves founded and supported theatres aimed at broad audiences. Besides Catherine the Great in Russia, the last Polish King Stanislaus Poniatowski opened the National Theatre in Warsaw as early as 1765 and the Habsburg Emperor Joseph II revived theatrical life in Vienna in 1776 by forming the Court and National Theatre (widely known as the Burgtheater ever since).

Although King Stanislaus was nurtured by the predominant French culture, he developed a lasting admiration for Shakespeare during his visit to England in 1754, as attested by his French *Memoirs*:

> Lord Strange was the first to take me to a performance of one of Shakespeare's tragedies. I took with me a vivid memory of all the beautiful rules of the unities of place, action and time, the minute observation of which gives the French dramatists their idea of their own superiority over the English. But I must admit that the more I became acquainted with the plays of Shakespeare, the less I began to believe in this supposed superiority. I felt involved, amused and more than once even edified: and I inferred from this that I might gain pleasure and even profit from seeing a play whose action lasts longer than one day and whose setting changes from one place to another, as long as the author possesses a thorough knowledge of the customs, passions, defects and even virtues of which people are capable.[1]

Preceding Tsarina Catherine the Great, the Polish King was able to change his taste and abandon the deep-rooted dramatic unities of French neoclassical drama in favour of Shakespeare's free structure and diction, which gave him more pleasure and satisfaction than 'the monotonously sublime, in fact, pompous style of the French tragedies'. He even translated *Julius Caesar* from Shakespeare's original into French, the language prevailing at his court.

Further appreciation of Shakespeare was spread in Poland by the influential periodical the *Monitor* which was based on English models and made good use of Samuel Johnson's common-sense criticism. Moreover, at least two Shakespearian adaptations originated in the *Monitor* group. One of them, *The Braggart or The Werewolf Lover* (pub. 1782), was a free translation of a jocular French adaptation of *The Merry Wives of Windsor*. It preceded Catherine the Great's Russian adaptation of the same play by four years. A German adaptation of the *Merry Wives* was performed in Vienna as early as 1771 under the title *The Merry Adventures in Vienna*.

At the National Theatre in Warsaw, Shakespeare was long performed only by German visiting companies (1775, 1781, 1793). It is all the more remarkable, then, that a Polish *Hamlet* was staged in 1798 in Lvov (Lemberg, in the Austrian part of occupied Poland). The translator was Wojciech Bogusławski, 'the father of the Polish theatre', who relied on a German prose version in eliminating most of the 'violent' action and reaching a happy ending with young Hamlet ascending the throne. Bogusławski himself took the title part and wrote a preface which shows how strong was the hold of French neoclassical theory on Poland even among the admirers of Shakespeare:

A long play that takes five hours to perform, a play that in disregarding the conventions of drama destroys the audience's interest; a play that, by present-ing on stage low characters and ugly scenes, cheapens tragic grandeur; a play, lastly, whose ending disregards all moral purpose, punishing the guilty as well as the innocent with death; such a play could not be staged in an enlightened era without necessary improvements. Still, it could hardly be neglected because of other undeniable beauties which only Shakespeare's genius could create and make immortal.

Bogusławski's *Hamlet*, reworked and performed several times dur-ing his lifetime, led to further Polish Shakespearian adaptations based mostly on German and occasionally French versions. Although the German influence on Polish culture was often resisted because of the Austrian and Prussian occupation of parts of Poland, progressive Ger-man art and thought continued to be accepted; for example, the national revivals in Poland and also in the Czech lands, Slovakia, and other Slavonic countries gathered strength and inspiration from the German philosopher, critic, and poet J. G. von Herder, whose *Outlines of the Philosophy of Man* (1784–91) hailed the resurrection of Slavonic nations as a major evolutionary force in the peaceful devel-opment of mankind.

A cultural situation similar to Poland's prevailed in the Czech lands. In Prague, Shakespeare was also performed for a long time only by the permanent German theatre founded in 1738 and noted for the first German performances of *Richard II* (1777) and *Timon of Athens* (1778). The Prague *Hamlet* in 1776 inspired F. L. Schröder to introduce the play to Hamburg in the same year. The success of the Hamburg production was so resounding that almost every theatre and wander-ing troupe in the German-speaking countries was gripped by a *Hamlet* mania.

As to Czech, it was spoken at that time mostly by the peasantry and patriotic clergy in the country and the lower middle class, servants, and patriotic intelligentsia in the towns. In 1781, however, Emperor Joseph

II's edicts opened new possibilities by abolishing serfdom and guaranteeing the defeated Protestants partial toleration. The very next year, two curious Czech chapbooks appeared in south Bohemia with the titles *The Merchant of Venice, or Love and Friendship* and *Macbeth, Leader of the Scottish Army*. Embellished by crude woodcuts on their title-pages, the little volumes named neither author nor translator but stated in their subtitles and short prefaces that they were translations from German 'comedies' and were offered to lovers of the Czech language who could not see the plays in Prague and other large towns. In the form of prose narratives they paraphrased the actions and speeches of the German adaptations of the two plays. Disarmingly naïve as the two anonymous narratives are, they are among the first tales from Shakespeare, preceding by a quarter of a century the famous *Tales* of Charles and Mary Lamb.

The first Shakespeare play in Czech was *Macbeth*, published in Prague in 1786 by K. H. Thám. In that year, a band of Czech patriots opened a playhouse known popularly as the 'Booth' on what is now St Wenceslas Square. Thám, the respected author of *A Defence of the Czech Language*, was the leading spirit of the 'patriots from the Booth', as they were called. In the preface to his translation, he recommended both reading and watching plays in Czech and appealed to patriotic well-to-do people to support activities which contributed 'not only to the spreading and improvement of the language but also to the enlightenment and education of the nation'. Obviously, Thám was professing the main tenets of the West European Enlightenment. At the same time, however, he and his compatriots were launching a courageous campaign of national and social revival. They wanted to prove to the whole nation and the world that the Czech language was capable of expressing the highest achievements of European dramatic art, even if they had to use inadequate or clumsy prose and some equally clumsy rhymes. Understandably, Thám's *Macbeth* was based on one of the German adaptations of the period. The rough scenes of the witches were shortened and softened by the addition of jumping male 'magicians' who were apparently regarded as more respectable. On the other hand, they remind us of the tumblers of the English Comedians and, ultimately, of the leapers in *The Winter's Tale*. In a final compliance with neoclassical taste, no severed head was presented victoriously at the end of the tragedy. Instead, Macduff took up the abandoned sword of dead Macbeth and asked Malcolm to step, as the rightful king, on the neck of the defeated tyrant. Tyranny was over, the time was free!

Like Karamzin's Russian translation of *Julius Caesar*, Thám's *Macbeth* aroused political anxiety among the authorities, who were alarmed by the recent events in America and France. In 1790 the title-pages of the remaining copies of the first Czech adaptation of Shakespeare were ordered to be torn out and the text to be sold as waste paper. Three more Czech Shakespearian adaptations from the same period suffered a similar fate. While the version of *King Lear* (performed 1792) survived at least in manuscript (pub. 1966), the first Czech adaptations of *Hamlet* (performed 1791) and *Romeo and Juliet* (performed 1805) have not been recovered.

National revivals sprang up also in the non-Slavonic countries of Eastern Europe. A good example is Hungary, which was also a restless and potentially subversive part of the Habsburg Empire. In the eighteenth century, the Hungarian language was spoken mostly by the peasants as well as by relatively small circles of hereditary nobility and patriotic intelligentsia. Shakespeare was introduced in German adaptations in the old Hungarian capital Buda (first recorded performance 1776) but also in Pozsony (now Bratislava, the capital of Slovakia, 1774) and Kassa (now Košice in east Slovakia). The predominantly Slovak rural and mountainous region in the north became important as the location of the last stand against the Turkish invasions in the sixteenth and seventeenth centuries, so it is not too surprising that the earliest Hungarian versions of Shakespeare were printed here. The first was *Romeo and Juliet*, published in Pozsony in 1786; the second, much more important, was *Hamlet*, which was brought out in Kassa in 1790. Both were free adaptations of German prose versions, but *Hamlet* was enriched by distinctly Hungarian, topical features which met with a wide and long-lasting success. Its author was Ferenc Kazinczy, a poet, critic, translator, and ardent organizer of a nationalist rehabilitation of the Hungarian language and literature.

Kazinczy introduced topical allusions from the very first scenes, which were dominated by the Ghost, representing not only the old King of Denmark but also the venerable past of Hungary destroyed by the usurping Habsburgian Claudius. Prince Hamlet was shaped by a number of cuts into an active and determined hero overcoming all obstacles by his will to revenge his adored father. His soliloquies were the only remnants of the hesitant, philosophizing bent of his mind. After killing Oldenholm (=Polonius), the Prince turned to Gusztáv (=Horatio) and insisted: 'Let's not waste time, Gusztáv, but take revenge for my murdered Father!' Bringing about a reconciliation with his repenting mother as well as with Laertes, he executed his revenge, addressed the court with 'You that look pale and tremble at this chance, report me and my cause aright to Denmark', and ascended the throne to prove most royally. In this way, Hamlet's succession was turned into an assertion of a just world order in which private losses were compensated by political success and the young hero, succeeding his murdered father, revived the spirit of the whole nation.

The topical significance of Kazinczy's *Hamlet* was stressed by his own preface in which he asked pathetically:

Who would not cry with joy when our destroyed, trampled-on Nation raises its head from the dust once again, and returning to its language, dress and mores, it will once again be what our Ancestors were, it will be what half a year ago the faint hope would not have believed; a free nation,—a Nation having its own constitution, language, and dress,—a Nation every member of which is born to carry a sword, and is a ready defender of his Country and his King.[2]

Kazinczy's great expectations were raised by the fact that the new Emperor, Leopold II, arrived in Buda in 1790 dressed in Hungarian national costume to be crowned king according to the old Hungarian constitution. The Hungarian national revival, however, was exposed to many more trials until 1867, when the Habsburgs made a compromise and ceded to the Hungarians, as the most consistently driving nationalist force in their empire, autonomous rule over the historic lands of the medieval Crown of St István (Hungary proper, Slovakia, Transylvania, Croatia, and Banat). Paradoxically, the Hungarian nationalists did not hesitate to suppress other nationalist movements within their domain more ruthlessly than the relenting Habsburgs.

To return to *Hamlet*, the victorious Prince prevailed in Hungary until 1839, when he was allowed to die for the first time in the new translation of Péter Vajda. This first Hungarian translation from the original was produced at the National Theatre, opened in Pest in 1837. A greatly superior rendering by the poet and critic János Arany was published in 1867, also in Pest, as part of the first complete edition of

Shakespeare in Hungarian (published in the years 1864–78). About the same period, the first editions of Shakespeare's complete works were also published in Czech (1855–72) and Polish (1875–7).

Although Vajda and Arany were hardly aware of it, their striving for an authentic Shakespeare had been preceded in the northern Slovak province by two Protestant ministers who translated *Hamlet* from the original into archaic biblical Czech tinged with current Slovak words (Slovak was codified as a literary language only by the middle of the nineteenth century). In 1806 Bohuslav Tablic published Hamlet's soliloquy 'To be or not to be' in a collection of his poems. In 1810, his younger, feisty colleague Michal Bosý, using the pen-name Bohuslav Křižák, translated the whole of *Hamlet*, and continued to improve on it occasionally for twenty years.

Both Tablic and Bosý had studied theology at the German University of Jena, as there was no Protestant theological college in the Habsburg Empire, and Bosý had become a student of A. W. von Schlegel, an outstanding scholar and translator, one of the pioneers of German Romantic interpretation of Shakespeare. Following both the theory and the practice of his teacher, Bosý translated *Hamlet* faithfully, using an unrhymed verse close to Shakespeare's blank verse as well as rhymes and prose when required by the original. Since there was no Slovak theatre at that time, Bosý's translation was meant much more as poetry than drama. As far as we know, it has never been performed and it became obsolete when the first Slovak professional theatres were founded after the First World War. A similar fate was destined for Bosý's translation of *The Two Gentlemen of Verona* and parts of *Macbeth*, although some excerpts were published in Slovak and Czech periodicals during the nineteenth century. Two manuscript fragments of Bosý's *Hamlet* (comprising Acts 1–2 and 4–5) were pieced together and published in Bratislava in 1964 as a contribution to the quatercentenary celebrations of Shakespeare's birth. The missing Act 3 was discovered and published as late as 1980.[3]

The Romantic movement brought not only the first adequate translations of Shakespeare but also a flowering of Shakespearian inspiration in East European drama, poetry, fiction, as well as music, painting, drawing, and sculpture. Although artistically not as outstanding as the Shakespearian drawings and paintings by Blake, Fuseli, or Delacroix, pictures of Shakespeare's characters and portraits and busts of Shakespeare himself gradually started to appear, arousing the reverence paid to religious icons.

Shakespeare's name became a cult word, calling forth the most abandoned flights of fancy. The most vigorous Hungarian Romantic poet, Sándor Petöfi (1822–49), wrote in 1847, two years before his premature death in the anti-Habsburg revolution of 1848–9: 'Shakespeare. Change his name into a mountain, and it will surpass the Himalayas; turn it into a sea, and you will find it broader and deeper than the Atlantic; convert it into a star, and it will outshine the sun itself... Before his appearance the world was incomplete, and when creating him God said: And behold him, oh, men, from now on you shall never doubt of my existence and greatness, if ever you dared to doubt!'[4] Petöfi's blending of traditional religious imagination with Byronic visions of Nature as a symbol of freedom was essentially different from the neoclassicist doctrine of nature as the source of 'order in variety' but it did not contradict Shakespeare's own representation of nature as alternately benevolent and wild.

Concurrently with his Shakespearian apotheosis, Petöfi joined forces with two other Hungarian poets, Mihály Vörösmarthy and János Arany, to translate Shakespeare's complete works. His premature death on the battlefield prevented him from translating more than one play, *Coriolanus* (pub. 1848), which was included along with Vörösmarthy's two and Arany's three translations in the first complete edition of Shakespeare's works mentioned above, and again, as classic translations, in the scholarly four-volume edition published in Budapest in 1955. Shakespeare's inspiration can be clearly seen in some of Petöfi's own poems, Vörösmarthy's plays, and Arany's epic and balladic poetry.

Perhaps the most creative Romantic response to Shakespeare in all of Eastern Europe developed in Poland. The coming of Polish Romanticism is usually connected with a volume of poems published in 1822 and entitled simply *Poesy*. It was introduced by an essay discussing the history of poetry and stressing the importance of old ballads and folk songs as a source of the new poetry of feeling and faith. The author of the volume, Adam Mickiewicz (1798–1855), was to become one of the major representatives of European Romanticism. Even Pushkin, with generous self-effacement, prized him above himself, and Belinsky called him 'one of the greatest poets of the world'.

Mickiewicz came from a family of Polish country gentry living rather modestly in the shifting borderland between Belarus and Lithuania, under the autocratic rule of the Russian tsars. As a youth of 14 he watched the proud but doomed march of Napoleon's army, reinforced with Polish legions, against Moscow. He enrolled in the distinguished Lithuanian University of Vilnius (Wilno) where he became active in a group of liberal and patriotic students. After graduating, he took up a teaching post and continued his education by reading Schiller, Goethe, German philosophy, Byron, Walter Scott, and Shakespeare, whom he studied with a dictionary in his hand. He also carried on his liberal political activities, for which he was banished from Lithuania in 1824 by order of the Tsar and transported to Russia to be more easily watched.

During his exile in St Petersburg, Odessa, and Moscow, he met liberal Russian intellectuals but in December 1825 he had to witness the defeat and the following cruel punishment of the Decembrist Rising. Translating Petrarch, Shakespeare, and Goethe in preparation for his own poetry, he wrote his own sequence of *Sonnets*, as well as ballads and narrative poems in which neoclassicist and Byronic influences were fused in a highly original manner. In two letters, sent in 1828 from St Petersburg to a fellow poet and playwright in Warsaw, he insisted that 'the only kind of drama answering the needs of our age is historical drama' and recommended, as the best models, Schiller, Goethe, and 'Shakespeare in particular'. In this view, Mickiewicz was close to Pushkin, whom he met briefly during his Russian exile. Finally, arousing the strong suspicions of the tsarist authorities, Mickiewicz was allowed to travel west; he lived in Germany, Switzerland, France, and Italy, and died in Constantinople (Istanbul), amid feverish preparations to form a Polish legion and fight the tsarist empire side by side with the Turkish, French, and British armies in the Crimean War. By an irony of fate, this great national poet never reached the Polish capital Warsaw, not even during the national uprising in 1830–1, although he was on the way there while it was being suppressed.

His most fertile periods were connected with Rome, Paris, and Dresden. In Paris, he published his free translation of an excerpt from *Romeo and Juliet*, starting with Juliet's soliloquy 'Gallop apace, you fiery-footed steeds' (3.2.1 ff.), which has been treasured as a jewel of Polish Shakespearian translation. Teaching a course on Slavonic literature as a professor at the Collège de France, Mickiewicz discussed Shakespeare in a highly Romantic fashion, adorning historical facts with his own poetic flights:

It is a well-known fact that Shakespeare's most imaginative scenes were performed in ruined buildings where there was no scenery or stage-machinery. Some of his works were even performed for the first time in sheds. But the magic of the English poet is so great that, even while we are reading them, we see light and shadows, ghosts and knights, castles rising up from the ground: the result of this is that the reader feels he is on the stage among the actors. (Lecture 16, 4 Apr. 1843)

Mickiewicz's masterpiece, the poetic drama *Forefathers' Eve* (*Dziady*), consists of typically Romantic fragments written partly in Vilnius (Parts I, II, and IV) and partly in Dresden (Part III). Part II is introduced by a slightly adapted motto from *Hamlet* (1.5.168–9), given both in the original and in Polish translation:

There are more things in heaven and earth, Horatio,
Than are dreamt of in our philosophy.

The motto is pertinent to the ensuing action which dramatizes the ancient, half-pagan, half-Christian custom of raising the spirits of dead forefathers and regaling them with food and drink on All Souls' Eve. Folklore motifs are combined with a spurned lover's mad fantasies about his lass's angelic beauty and torturing frailty. Since he has committed suicide, the dead lover returns to the world as, successively, a vampire, a hunter, and a pilgrim. Part III, valued by George Sand above Goethe's *Faust* and Byron's *Manfred*, is distinguished by an immense richness of metrical forms, rhyming patterns, and poetic visions in which mystical outbursts of Titanism and messianism are succeeded by religious humility and realistic pictures of the persecution of young patriots by a drunken, beastly tsarist senator in Vilnius. The Shakespearian inspiration is completely absorbed but can be felt in the free dramatic structure, where scenes from different parts of Lithuania, Poland, and Russia follow each other without any spatial or temporal barriers, in the fusion of folk elements with original imagery, and in the poetic exploration of the undiscovered country between the natural and supernatural world from whose bourn the ghosts of the dead visit the living. In many scenes of Part III Hamlet's vision of Denmark as a prison underlines the fate of Polish patriots in Lithuania.

Mickiewicz demanded that Polish drama should not imitate any foreign model but rather emulate the spirit of Shakespeare. In this insistence he was followed by his compatriot and greatest rival Juliusz Słowacki (1809–49), the chief creator of a substantial body of poetic drama. Słowacki also studied at the University of Vilnius but, being younger and belonging to a family of higher Polish gentry who were not opposed to the tsarist regime, he missed the liberal student movement of Mickiewicz's generation and joined the patriotic agitation much later, during the outburst of the Polish national uprising in 1830. He did not take part in the actual fighting, however, as he was sent from Warsaw to London on a diplomatic mission to win support for the provisional revolutionary government. Like Mickiewicz, he did not take up arms against the occupation powers directly and suffered for the rest of his life from twinges of conscience for having evaded the enemy when honour was at stake.

While in London, Słowacki came under the spell of Shakespeare in 1831 when he had the good luck to see the 'incomparable' Edmund Kean 'in his most famous role, i.e. Richard III', as he wrote to his mother. His admiration for Shakespeare resulted partly in his translations of excerpts from *King Lear* and *Macbeth* but mainly in his own verse plays. The excerpt from *King Lear* was incorporated in *Kordian* (pub. in Paris 1834), in which the young title hero, bearing an unmistakable resemblance to his author, decides to commit suicide out of unhappy love but finds escape and consolation in travelling to the West. After a visit to London he appears sitting on the white cliffs of Dover, reading aloud Edgar's description of the fearful precipice (*King Lear*, 4.5.11–24). Kordian muses on the fate of man, comparing it to the dreadful trade of the poor wretch who hangs and gathers samphire on the cliffs of life. Kordian's travels culminate on the highest peak of Mont Blanc where he finds a new perspective in the love of his native country.

In Act 3, Count Kordian comes to Warsaw to join a conspiracy against Tsar Nicholas I during his coronation as king of Poland. On the very threshold of the Tsar's bedroom, however, he swoons, succumbing to the tension between his will to kill the tyrant and the feeling of guilt resulting from the action. He is put in a lunatic asylum, and the question arises whether, like Hamlet, he is 'mad in craft' or in reality. Finally, he is condemned to death by the Tsar but Grand Duke

Constantine, the Tsar's brother, wins a last-minute reprieve for him. In the dramatic concluding scene, Kordian stands before the execution squad, and the commanding officer is raising his hand at the same time that the reprieve is being brought by a galloping aide-de-camp. The baffled crowd accompanies the action with cries of pity and fear. Originally, the play was planned as a trilogy, so that this first part has remained a fragment, like many other works of Romantic poetry. As it stands, its action stops at the most stirring moment of the catastrophe, leaving us in suspense as to whether Kordian's life was saved or taken.

Similar appropriation of Shakespeare's heroes can be seen in the neo-Romantic fiction of Henryk Sienkiewicz (1846–1916), the contemporary of Joseph Conrad (another Pole by birth), and winner of the Nobel Prize for 1905. Particularly in his trilogy of historical novels *With Fire and Sword, The Deluge,* and *Pan Michael,* Sienkiewicz created subtle amalgams of Polish personalities of the seventeenth century with characters like Falstaff, Hotspur, or Henry V. In his homage to Shakespeare published in 1916, on the tercentenary of Shakespeare's death and in the year of his own death, he reflected: 'Shakespeare, after God, is the most mighty creator of souls. Therefore he dominates time and event . . . I will not multiply examples, yet it is a fact that Falstaff had in Poland a brother named Zagłoba, and that both have brothers living at this hour in England and in Poland—but the Polish brothers have grown so thin to-day that they are only shadows of their former selves.' This was an ironic reference to the severe famine in Poland during the First World War, a disaster inflicted all too often on this corn-producing country.

From the many outstanding East European actors and actresses whose highest ambition was to impersonate Shakespeare's characters, at least one more name should be added to the two Russian actors, Mochalov and Kachalov, singled out in the previous chapter. The Polish actress Helena Modrzejewska (1844–1909) excelled first in Warsaw in the years 1868–76 but achieved worldwide fame only after her emigration to the United States. There and also in England, Scotland, and Ireland she acted under the simplified name of Modjeska in such tragic roles as Ophelia, Lady Macbeth, Cleopatra, Juliet, and Desdemona. She was considered comparable to Sarah Bernhardt but she wisely resisted the temptation to play Hamlet *en travesti,* as the French star did at the age of 65.

It would be somewhat repetitive to discuss at length the national revivals in the rest of Eastern Europe where they usually set in somewhat later and developed in similar ways, with individual features displayed in each country. The vampire homeland of Transylvania (now north-west Romania) received Shakespeare a whole century before it was put on the literary map by Bram Stoker's *Dracula* (1897). By the end of the eighteenth century, Transylvania belonged to the Habsburg Empire, and, consequently, Shakespeare arrived there in German garb. The Transylvanian trade and cultural centre Kolozsvár (now Cluj) had a thriving German theatre with actors who had made their names in Vienna. Besides that, German, Hungarian, and, later on, Romanian troupes toured in the region. The first Hungarian specimen of Shakespeare, an excerpt from *Richard II* based on a German prose version, was published in Kolozsvár as early as 1785, and the first Hungarian performances of *Hamlet*, in the notable version of Ferenc Kazinczy, took place there in 1793 and 1794.

South of the Carpathians, in Wallachia, Shakespeare and his republican hero Brutus were embraced by the forerunners and leaders of the ill-fated anti-Habsburg revolution of 1848: *Julius Caesar* was published in Bucharest in 1844 as the first complete Romanian translation. It was based on a French version, since Romanian is essentially a Romance language in which the Latin foundation has been enriched by Greek, Turkish, Slavonic, German, and Hungarian elements. In 1850, a Romanian *Macbeth* was published, translated from French, but in 1864 it appeared again in the first Romanian translation from the original. By that time, the Romanian national revival was in full swing, and the tercentenary of Shakespeare's birth was celebrated by a whole garland of lectures and essays. Romanian theatre received a strong impetus in the years 1877–9 from the visit of the Italian actor Ernesto Rossi who fascinated audiences in Bucharest and other Romanian towns with his Othello, King Lear, Macbeth, Hamlet, and Richard III. In that period, Romania was reaching for full independence and in 1881 it was proclaimed a kingdom.

Among the Yugoslavs, the first admirer of Shakespeare, as far as we know, was the Slovene poet and playwright A. T. Linhart (1756–95). He attended Shakespearian performances at the Burgtheater in Vienna in 1778 and, under their influence, wrote his own drama in German, *Miss Jenny Love*, calling it, in a letter to a friend, 'as dark as

Shakespeare'. Two years later, on his return to his native country under the Alps, in the north-west of the Balkan Peninsula, he became dissatisfied with the fashionable revisions and distortions of Shakespeare, as they were performed in the German theatre of the Slovene capital Ljubljana, and called for Shakespeare's originals to be read, translated, and performed. His call could be answered only after the national revival of the Romantic period, when the Slovene translations were done and partly printed in 1864, again as a contribution to the tercentenary celebrations of Shakespeare's birth. The Slovene *Hamlet*, dating from that year, was performed only in 1899. It was preceded by the first Slovene production of *Othello* in Ljubljana in 1896.

Slovenia, governed by the Habsburgs, was close to the large Adriatic port Trieste, which was also a part of the Habsburg Empire until 1918. Before the First World War, Shakespeare was performed in Trieste not only in German and Italian but also in the professional Slovene theatre which offered *Hamlet* in 1908, presented by a visiting Croatian company, and three plays in Slovene between 1910 and 1914: *The Merchant of Venice*, *Othello*, and *Romeo and Juliet*. If we remember that James Joyce taught English in Trieste in those years, we must wonder whether he did not hear Shakespeare also in Slovene or Croatian. We know for certain that he saw the celebrated Italian actor Tommaso Salvini playing Hamlet in Trieste by the beginning of 1908 and that he was a passionate theatre-goer, hatching his own play *Exiles*. Although he preferred Ibsen to Shakespeare, he was always provoked by 'the Swan of Avon', as is copiously reflected in *Ulysses*, then in progress. His interest in Slovene and other Slavonic languages is best revealed in *Finnegans Wake*.

The most gifted and dedicated translator of Shakespeare into Slovene was the poet Oton Župančič (1878–1949), who did his first versions before the First World War, when Joyce was in Trieste, and continued to revise them and add new translations until he supplied the Slovene National Theatre in Ljubljana, where he became the managing director, with more than half of Shakespeare's canon.

The Croats, after the flowering of their Renaissance literature and drama in the Dalmatian port Dubrovnik, had to fight the Turks on the one hand and, on the other, to resist continuing attempts at Germanization or Hungarization as subjects of the Austro-Hungarian Empire. In the Croatian capital Zagreb, adaptations of Shakespeare in German were performed from the end of the eighteenth century. Perhaps the most noteworthy was the complete reshaping of *Hamlet* into *Eugenius Skokko, Erbprinz von Dalmatien* (1802), with the Prince of Denmark translated into the hereditary Prince of Dalmatia. The first recorded Croatian performance of Shakespeare took place in Zagreb in 1841. It was *Romeo and Juliet*, based on a widely popular German prose adaptation.

Serbo-Croatian was formed and reformed as a literary language in the first half of the nineteenth century by scholars and writers educated mostly in Austria or Hungary (Vienna, Graz, Pest) and inspired, like the West Slavs, by the Romantic movement in their search for and revival of their ethnic identities. In particular, they were fired by the victorious anti-Ottoman War of Independence of the Greeks (1821–32), so self-sacrificingly supported by Lord Byron. Among the Serbs, who had to survive partly in the Ottoman and partly in the Habsburg Empire, the first translator of Shakespeare was Laza Kostić (1841–1910), a poet of considerable originality and daring. He started to render Shakespeare into regular iambic pentameters of his mother-tongue as a very young man, so that his compatriots called him proudly 'our young Shakespeare'. In 1864 he took the leading part in the Serbian tercentenary celebrations of Shakespeare's birth, during which his poem on Shakespeare was read and the first act of his translation of *Richard III* was performed. In his first tragedy *Maksim Crnojević* (1866), he based the plot on a Serbian folk song, combining it with the philosophical reflections of the title hero, whose resemblance to Hamlet is endearing. After the liberation of Beograd in 1867 and the victorious anti-Ottoman rising of the Balkan Slavs in 1875–6, followed by the final defeat of the Turks in the Russo-Turkish wars of 1877–8, the way was opened for a full development of Slavonic literatures and theatre arts.

We can see a similar development also in Bulgaria, where *Romeo and Juliet* appeared upon an amateur stage as early as 1856 and again in a cultural club in 1868, apparently because a love play was more likely to be tolerated by Ottoman authorities. In 1880, when Turkish censorship was gone, *Julius Caesar* was published with a preface by the Bulgarian translator Ivan Slaveikov, who introduced Shakespeare, in glowing terms, for the first time to the Bulgarian reading public and stated that he had started his work five years ago, i.e. still under the Ottoman regime, and reworked it three times. His unusually conscientious rendering was based on the original, and although he translated into prose, occasionally he succeeded in catching the rhythm of Shakespeare's blank verse. Between 1881 and 1900 thirty-five Bulgarian versions of Shakespeare's plays were brought out. Most of them were not translated from the original but from the Russian, though German, French, Romanian, or Czech renderings were sometimes also consulted.

Last but not least comes Shakespearian inspiration in East European music. As early as 1776, the Czech musician Jiří Benda (1722–95), who was with many of his compatriots in the service of German aristocratic patrons, composed one of the early examples of a new musical genre called *Singspiel*, a type of light opera with spoken dialogue (a simplified version of the 'English opera', brought to perfection by Henry Purcell, and a precursor of Gilbert and Sullivan's operettas and modern musicals). It was called *Romeo and Juliet* and used a German libretto which provided Shakespeare's tragedy with a happy reunion of the young lovers, as expected at that time. Benda's music, however, was far from conventional, offering a lively richness of rhythmic and melodic variations in individual arias, duets, and choruses. It was well received and produced, after its première in Gotha, in many other places, including Prague (1783 and, in Czech translation, in 1931 and again in 1943, during the Nazi occupation of Bohemia). In the nineteenth century, it was overshadowed by the Italian and French operas (Vincenzo Bellini, Charles Gounod) and by Hector Berlioz's dramatic symphony, all on the same subject.

Finally, the Russian composer Peter Tchaikovsky (1840–93) took great pains with his fantasy overture *Romeo and Juliet* (1869, revised 1870, final version 1880), which integrated the dramatic and lyrical elements of Shakespeare's tragedy into a compact and forcefully graduated musical structure dominated by the theme of violent hatred counterbalanced and finally overcome by redeeming love. Two more orchestral works were composed by Tchaikovsky to form a Shakespearian triptych of great charm. The 'symphonic fantasy' *The Tempest* (1873) started and ended with the musical image of the sea and introduced another love theme, with Miranda and Ferdinand, surrounded by the musing of the sage Prospero, the fluttering of the airy spirit of Ariel, and the clumsy bounding the grotesque monster

Caliban. Tchaikovsky's other fantasy overture *Hamlet* (1888) repeated the successful formula of *Romeo and Juliet* by contrasting tragic and lyric features but invented some deeper, more meditative, more subdued passages concluded by the martial march of Fortinbras and the funeral march of the tragic hero. When asked by his theatre friends to compose incidental music to a forthcoming production of *Hamlet* in St Petersburg (1891), Tchaikovsky complied evidently in great haste, using both his *Hamlet* overture and pieces from his earlier works and adding some new parts, such as an overture to Act 3 and more music for Ophelia.

Among other East European Romantic and post-Romantic Shakespearian composers at least two stand out with undeniable originality. The phenomenal Hungarian pianist and composer Ferenc or Franz Liszt (1811–86) was active in the west of Europe for most of his life but his native temperament remained evident in both his playing and composing. He originated the genre of the symphonic poem and concluded a whole series of them by *Hamlet* (1859), a musical study of the enigmatic Prince, very much in harmony with the Romantic probing into Shakespeare's characters rather than action. In comparison with the *Hamlet* of Tchaikovsky, Liszt's composition is more concentrated on the hero's soliloquies, starting with 'To be or not to be' and expressing his wavering by subtle transitions from one key to another.

Liszt was one of the first to appreciate and encourage Bedřich Smetana (1824–84), the chief founder of the Czech national school but also a lifelong admirer of Shakespeare. One of his earliest orchestral compositions was the symphonic poem *Richard III* (1858) which represented the hunchbacked king not only in his halting, uneven walk but also in his inner tension, his daredevil drive towards the highest goal, his horrifying dream before the final battle, and his defeat. Next year, Smetana composed a virtuoso piano piece called *Macbeth and the Witches*, a highly dramatic rendering of Macbeth's final encounter with the weird sisters who dance to a grotesque devil's polka and gloat over their double-sense prophecy. The second part of the composition captures Macbeth's dreadful reign of terror followed by his final desperate fight and fall.

In 1864, Smetana became the central figure in the Prague tercentenary celebrations of Shakespeare's birth. Preceded by a cycle of five

Shakespearian performances, the Jubilee itself was conceived as a composite work of art, consisting of music, poetry, singing, acting, painting, and sculpture. It took place in the largest theatre hall in central Prague and was opened by Berlioz's *Romeo and Juliet* conducted by Smetana. A poetic prologue was recited by a famous actor dressed as Prospero. Six *tableaux vivants* with background music represented scenes from all of Shakespeare's dramatic genres: one comedy, one history, two tragedies, and two romances. The climax was reached when Smetana's heroic *Shakespearian March*, freshly composed for the occasion, accompanied the procession of almost 250 characters from Shakespeare's plays dressed in historical costumes and slowly passing under a large bust of the poet created by the most promising young Czech sculptor of the day. The characters were represented not only by actors, some performing short scenes, but also by prominent patriotic citizens (Falstaff was impersonated by Prague's stoutest butcher). Finally the procession settled around Shakespeare's bust to listen to the poetic epilogue of the alleged Bohemian shepherdess Perdita from the *Winter's Tale*. Represented by a popular actress, she embodied both Shakespeare's 'fair Bohemia' and Bohemian art (Perdita Ars Bohemica) which was lost after the Habsburg victory over the Bohemian estates in 1618 but was revived and fully restored now to become an equal partner of all European nations. Fortunately, the Jubilee procession was permanently preserved in six oil paintings by Karel Purkyně (1834–68) who also designed four of the *tableaux vivants*, joining Smetana as the chief creator of the whole event. Although the Prague Shakespearian Jubilee of 1864 may appear today as a rather flamboyant outburst of Czech nationalist spirit, there can be no doubt about its high cultural level and political significance. If the Czechs were often denied the possibility of fighting for their independence, they never ceased in their striving to reach the level of the most cultured nations of Europe.

In the years 1873–4, Smetana started to compose his opera *Viola*, based on *Twelfth Night*, to which he returned in the last year of his life, deaf and fatally ill, to find consolation in Shakespeare's poetry and humour. But his dream about a Shakespearian comic opera to form a lyric counterpart to his frolicsome *Bartered Bride* remained a shining fragment (less than one act). It has been revived from time to time and offered the Czechs special consolation during the Nazi occupation of

Bohemia and Moravia, when it was produced at the Prague National Theatre in 1944 as part of a Smetana programme that was suppressed immediately after its first night.

It would take too long to give a full account of the Czech artistic tributes to Shakespeare, so that two further examples must suffice. In 1892, Antonín Dvořák (1841–1904) composed his concert overture *Othello*, a highly dramatic piece which should be enjoyed for its general musical intensity without trying to find exact parallels to the details of Shakespeare's tragedy. In 1911, the Czech sculptor Otto Gutfreund (1881–1927) created a unique Cubist statue of Hamlet (now a permanent exhibit in the Prague Gallery of Modern Art), presenting the Prince in stark but elegant pose, strikingly without arms, to express his helplessness against a sea of troubles, but with a burden on his left

Fig. 2. Hamlet, sculpture by Otto Gutfreund

shoulder, to suggest the reason for his weariness. For all that, the lonely hero with a meditative face, firm chin, long neck, and protruding left side of his chest creates the impression of a noble heart gathering energy for resistance. One moves in awe and excitement around this slight figure (70 cm in height) who was holding his little patch of ground a mere three years before the outbreak of the First World War, on the threshold of the most destructive and self-destructive era in human history.

FURTHER READING

Stanisław Helsztyński (ed.), *Poland's Homage to Shakespeare, Commemorating the Fourth Centenary of his Birth 1564–1964* (Warsaw, 1965), has a number of essays in English discussing the reception of Shakespeare in Poland. In Czechoslovakia, a similar volume entitled *Charles University on Shakespeare*, edited by Zdeněk Stříbrný, was published in Prague in 1966. A Shakespeare Memorial Number of the *New Hungarian Quarterly*, 5/13, edited by Iván Boldizsár, appeared in spring 1964 in Budapest. Further valuable essays in English are in the *Shakespeare Yearbook*, vol. 8, edited by Holgar Klein and Péter Dávidházi under the title *Shakespeare and Hungary* (Lewiston, NY, 1996). Alexandru Duţu's thorough monograph *Shakespeare in Rumania* (Bucharest, 1964) was followed by his article 'Recent Shakespeare Performances in Romania', *Shakespeare Survey 20* (1967). A short historical survey 'Shakespeare and Yugoslavia' by Hugo Klajn was published in *Shakespeare Quarterly*, 5 (1954). In France Kotlar (ed.), *Shakespeare pri Slovencih* (Ljubljana, 1965), essays in Slovene are provided with good English summaries. A collection of essays in English and French, *European Shakespeares: Translating Shakespeare in the Romantic Age*, edited by Dirk Delabastita and Lieven D'hulst (Amsterdam, 1993), is thought-provoking.

4

Shakespeare after the
Bolshevik Revolution

I

The Bolshevik Revolution in October 1917 and the following Civil War between the Red Army and the Whites (tsarist armies supported by foreign legions, 1918–20) led to a massive emigration of the Russian aristocracy, the army élite, and part of the intelligentsia, including a number of actors, directors, and designers. One of the most successful was Fedor Komissarzhevsky (1882–1954), a director-cum-designer who became well known in the West as Theodore Komisarjevsky, or simply Komis, as he was named by friends and fans. The only Shakespeare play Komisarjevsky designed and directed in Russia was *The Tempest*, staged at the Novy (New) Theatre in Moscow in 1919. It was obviously inspired by the MAT *Hamlet*, especially Gordon Craig's 'synthetic theatre', combining mystical and symbolic interpretation of the text with a modern Constructivist set evolved from Cubism. Tall white boxes and an indented staircase provided an abstract space for Prospero's philosophical musing, Caliban's grotesque revolt, and Ariel's stylized postures and high leaps aspiring to the very tops of the sets. Similar staging devices, enriched by expressionist German and experimental British features, were to be used by Komisarjevsky in England, where he arrived within the same year.

After a preliminary experiment with *King Lear* at the Oxford University Drama Society in 1927, Komisarjevsky drew much attention by his productions of both tragedies and comedies at the Shakespeare Memorial Theatre at Stratford-upon-Avon 1932–9. Heated controversy was aroused by his 'steel' or 'aluminium' *Macbeth* (1933), located on a Constructivist set of gigantic steel shields and burnished aluminium staircases with added scrollwork, the whole scene fired by thunder and lightning or infused with an ominous cold sheen. Macbeth, reminiscent of a German officer of the First World War, met the witches, old Scottish fortune-tellers plundering corpses on the battle-field, against the background of a bombed-out building. There were other visual references to the First World War: the military uniforms of the soldiers and an abandoned howitzer upstage in the final battle scene. If we look at the preserved photographs, close affinities between the Moscow *Tempest* and the Stratford *Macbeth* become apparent.

Komisarjevsky's productions in the West belong to the history of British, American, and Canadian theatre. Here it must suffice to say that he was largely instrumental in preparing the ground for the revolution in British theatre in the second half of the twentieth century. His Stratford *King Lear* (1936) opened the way for the forceful production of the tragedy by another director of East European back-ground, Peter Brook (1962, film version 1969). In the genre of comedy too Komisarjevsky's contribution was seminal. His Stratford *Comedy of Errors* (1938–9) has been evaluated by theatre historians as a major production of the century, and its inventiveness in fast-paced physical action, song, and dance issued a challenge to the subsequent free versions of the comedy in the United States and the United Kingdom, including the Stratford revival (1963), which turned out to be the play's most popular production in history. Appropriately, during the Shake-speare quatercentenary in 1964, both Peter Brook's *King Lear* and Clifford Williams's *Comedy of Errors* were brought to Prague and other East European cities by the Royal Shakespeare Company. Peter Brook stated that his *King Lear* was received much more intensely between Budapest and Moscow than in the West.

A less fortunate 'wandering star', as the émigrés were called meta-phorically, was the actor Michael Chekhov (1891–1955), nephew of the famous writer and dramatist. In 1924–5 the Moscow Art Theatre II (a studio of the main theatre) produced another *Hamlet*, with Michael Chekhov in the title role, which provoked widely different critical evaluations. Recent research by both Russian and Western scholars has shown that Chekhov's unusual erudition enriched his portrait of the Prince with psychological insights based on Dostoevsky, early Russian existentialism, and German anthroposophy, an occult teaching about the union of philosopher and philosophy, of body, soul, and spirit. Theatrically oriented critics have observed Chekhov's connections with Craig and Stanislavsky's 'spirit vs. matter' MAT *Hamlet* of 1911–12 as well as the symbolic and expressionistic *Hamlets* (1909, 1910, 1913, 1920) of the Austrian director Max Reinhardt who was mostly active in Berlin.

Official Communist critics, however, immediately branded Chekhov's interpretation as decadent and reactionary. Evidently, they could not endure the 'suffering and deathly horror in his eyes' as he moved 'with nervous, wavering steps to meet his doom'. Although he emphasized his duty of revenge, 'he appeared so crushed by grief and despair for himself and mankind that his consciousness seemed to disintegrate'. After an outburst of activity in the last scene, culminating in the killing of Claudius, Hamlet accepted his own death peacefully, with a lucid mind, 'as if carefully laying his body by'. 'The more impotent Hamlet's body became, the brighter and more all-consuming became his inner life, which was abetted by the stage lighting.'[1]

Growing Bolshevik pressure finally forced Chekhov to defect from the Soviet Union in 1928. In his letter to the Czechoslovak President T. G. Masaryk he explained his decision in restrained but determined terms:

External influences of a tendentious system of inspection and the narrowly propagandistic demands of the censorship in Russia have deprived the artist of freedom in the area of his creative activity. However, there is still much strength, and many artistic projects and cultural aspirations dwelling in the souls of those who were raised and educated within the walls of the Art Theatre. . . . I want to save the wonderful theatrical culture which once inspired me and gave me life as an artist. I want to serve the further flourishing and development of those precepts which I received from my teacher Konstantin Sergeevich Stanislavsky.[2]

Wandering through the European Continent, England, and finally America, Chekhov directed, acted, and taught acting in dramatic art schools which he founded in England and, after 1939, in the United States. He educated many devoted and some outstanding disciples (including Gregory Peck, Yul Brynner, and Marilyn Monroe) but he was never given the full opportunity to confirm his potential as a great actor. His quirky desperadoes in Hollywood B-movies were a far cry from his fascinating Moscow Hamlet.

Chekhov's mentor Konstantin Stanislavsky (1863–1938) did some wandering, too, but much of the time he preferred to stick it out in his native country. In 1922–4 he headed a group of MAT actors on their long tour of Europe and two visits to the United States, while the co-founder of the MAT, Nemirovich-Danchenko, was warily guarding the nest in Moscow. Between performances on tour, Stanislavsky managed to write one of the most influential books on acting, *My Life in Art* (published first in Boston, 1924, then in Moscow, 1926, and many other cities of the world), to which he later added several books explaining in more detail his method of training actors in rich psychological development and simple external expression of characters.

Although the MAT performances in the United States were warmly appreciated by both audiences and most critics, the yellow press attacked them as Bolshevik propaganda. This was a ludicrous accusation because all the plays performed were chosen from the pre-Revolution MAT repertoire with special stress on Anton Chekhov, the playwright revealed by the company to the world, including the New World. In fact, it was remarkable how the MAT, both abroad and at home, stuck to their guns in choosing and performing their plays. As the official Communist insistence on socialist realism was escalating, the MAT introduced new Soviet authors, adding them to their old choice, Maxim Gorky, 'the stormy petrel of the Revolution', whom they had performed since 1902. While the chief Bolshevik leader V. I. Lenin taught fervently that there were two cultures in each national culture, the reactionary culture of the exploiters and the progressive culture of the exploited, Stanislavsky stated quietly that there were only two kinds of art for him: good and bad.

As far as Shakespeare was concerned, both Stanislavsky and Nemirovich-Danchenko were striving to build on their pre-Revolution productions of *Julius Caesar* and *Hamlet*. Stanislavsky himself had tackled Shakespeare even before his MAT career. In 1896, he directed *Othello* in Moscow, taking the title part, as an imposing period photograph demonstrates. He was the first Othello to bring roses for Desdemona, inspiring Laurence Olivier and many other actors of the twentieth century.

In 1929–30, he returned to *Othello* with great zest to prepare a new production at the MAT. Unfortunately, his deteriorating health forced him to depart for a cure at Nice on the French Riviera, where he wrote detailed scene-by-scene notes which were used for rehearsals in Moscow and published much later under the title *A Plan for Staging Othello* (Moscow, 1945, English translation 1948 under the title *Stanislavsky Rehearses Othello*). Although unfinished (the notes end with Act 4, Scene 1), the *Plan* offers not only detailed discussions of individual characters and scenes, accompanied by many drawings of *mise-en-scène*, but also a fairly consistent interpretation of the whole tragedy. It is important to realize that this interpretation was based on Stanislavsky's own experience from as far back as the end of the nineteenth century, when his first creative encounter with Shakespeare was strongly influenced by the Italian guest actor Tommaso Salvini who had fascinated Moscow with his late Romantic Othello in 1891.

Another early experience used by Stanislavsky in his *Plan* was the MAT production of *Julius Caesar* in 1903 (as described at the end of Chapter 2). Whereas *Othello* had often been seen primarily as a domestic tragedy, Stanislavsky took great pains to plan the action on a large background of clashing political and social forces, including the threat of a people's revolt, recalling the rising of the plebeians in *Julius Caesar*. To achieve this, he had to imagine that in Act 2, when the action moved to Cyprus, the Cypriots were Turkish people suffering under the yoke of Venice and ready to rise as soon as the Turkish fleet arrived to liberate them. This highly speculative threat of revolt was misused by Iago who not only provoked the fight between the drunken Cassio and Montano but schemed to incite and suppress a Cypriot rising to make Cassio's brawl look much more serious and dangerous. The attention paid to the Cypriot populace by the MAT production is amply illustrated by the colourful oriental costumes designed for nine different natives and reproduced in the *Plan*. In short, the MAT production was planned to be thoroughly historical in background and neo-Romantic in the conception of characters. It aimed at showing great social contradictions inherent in the Renaissance epoch which produced such pure, warm-hearted, idealistic heroes as Othello and Desdemona but also such villainous individualists, reckless careerists, and large-scale schemers as Iago.

For all these painstaking preparations, the actual MAT production of *Othello* (1930) was not a great success. None the less, it started a long series of *Othellos* all over the vast spaces of the Soviet Union; for several decades, *Othello* was all the rage, being performed not only in Russian but also in Georgian, Armenian, Tajik, Uzbek, Chuvach—altogether in sixteen languages. The Armenian actor Vagram Papazian played Othello first in 1908 and continued performing the role in Armenian, Russian, Italian, and French. When he brought his Othello to Paris in 1932, audiences were reportedly 'moved to tears' and one Paris newspaper declared that the part seemed to have been written for him. Altogether, he played Othello more than 3,000 times!

A widely acclaimed and influential production of *Othello* opened at the Moscow Maly (Small) Theatre by the end of 1935 under the direction of Sergei Radlov in the new translation of his wife Anna Radlova. The part of Othello was taken by Alexander Ostuzhev, an old-established actor who had joined the Maly ensemble in 1898 and played Cassio in 1900, supporting Tommaso Salvini on his guest return to Moscow.

Ostuzhev decided to counterbalance Othello's fiery temper with gentleness of heart and purity of soul symbolized by his white costume. One of the critics compared him to 'the grieved Moor made jealous by a slave' (as Richard Burbage, the chief tragedian of Shakespeare's company, was commemorated in a funeral elegy on his death in 1619). Ostuzhev's Othello was not jealous by nature, he was made jealous by Iago, who envied him his splendid military career and happiness in personal life. Building on an old Russian tradition reaching back to Pushkin's insight that Othello was not fundamentally jealous but trustful, the whole production was interpreted as a tragedy of betrayed trust rather than a tragedy of jealousy. Othello killed Desdemona not in a paroxysm of passion but as a man crushed by grief, convinced that he was executing a stern act of justice to destroy a source of evil. When he finally discovered that Desdemona was innocent, he wept for joy in his renewed faith in mankind and destroyed himself as the real source of evil for having surrendered his humanistic ideals to Iago's vicious inhumanity. The role of Iago was updated to include the racist tendencies of 'these days when chauvinism is again on the loose, preached by the medieval fanatics in the Fascist countries and also in some bourgeois-democratic countries of the capitalist world'.

This is what Ostuzhev felt in 1938 when the Nazis, in alliance with Italian Fascists, were preparing their conquest of Europe. The situation was so dangerous that Ostuzhev and other artists in the Soviet Union were willing to ignore silently or even endorse Stalin's totalitarian terror, culminating in the monstrous political trials, executions, and massive deportations. It is with a sense of colossal discrepancy between utopian illusion and cruel reality that we now read with hindsight Ostuzhev's idealized image of Soviet society: 'The Soviet people love Othello, as I do, because we love man. Life in our country is devoted to ensuring through all its policies the realization of a society which will care for man, for people, and teach the love of man. . . . We detest Iago because, on the road of Othello, on the road of man and on our road, there lurk venomous reptiles who hide their poisoned fangs under a hypocritical mask.'[3]

Whereas *Othello* was being wholeheartedly embraced by both Soviet theatres and critics, the approach to *Hamlet* became so cautious and sometimes evasive that it can be perhaps best described as beating about the bush. The bush was dark and full of mysteries, problems, and questions so that it could not be straightforwardly correlated to the streamlined Soviet ideology. Added to the devastating critical attacks on Michael Chekhov's Hamlet, rumours were being spread by Communist apparatchiks that Stalin himself hated Hamlet, the crazy intellectual who did not know whether to be or not to be. In such an ambience, it was a brilliant idea of the Vakhtangov Theatre in Moscow to present an entirely iconoclastic, grotesque *Hamlet* in 1932.

Eugene Vakhtangov (1883–1922), a member of the pre-revolutionary MAT, was put in charge of the experimental MAT studio (MAT II) which almost immediately distinguished itself in 1921 by an avant-garde production of *Macbeth* with Vakhtangov in the title role. The studio continued developing the widest possible range of theatrical forms and was officially named after its founder four years after his death. It was clearly in Vakhtangov's spirit, especially his predilection for the grotesque, that director and designer Nikolai Akimov (1901–68) staged *Hamlet* as a zany play of political intrigue and struggle for the throne of Denmark.

The Prince soon turned out to be a clever manipulator, as he himself, speaking into an earthen jar, pretended to be his father's Ghost in order to win adherents for his conflict with Claudius.

Horatio was an accomplice to this deception, shouting at Marcellus in imitation of the Ghost: 'Swear.' When Horatio overdid it the fourth time and there was a danger that even the simple-minded soldier might guess what was really cooking, Hamlet gave Horatio a kick and calmed him down with 'Rest, rest, perturbèd spirit' (*Hamlet*, 1.5.183). During his central soliloquy, Hamlet sat in a tavern with a tall tumbler of wine in front of him and a paper crown on his head, indicating that his real question was whether to be or not to be king. His pretended madness came into full view in a market place where he paraded in a nightshirt, a paper rose in his hand, and a frying pan ornamented with a carrot on his head, leading a sucking-pig on a string. A dissipated Ophelia, apparently in allusion to Chekhov's Okhmelia in *The Cherry Orchard*, became so drunk that her drowning appeared pretty natural. Grotesque features were enriched with incidental music by Dmitri Shostakovich, for instance in the scene of Hamlet's conversation with his fellow students Rosencrantz and Guildenstern, whom he reproached with trying to play on him as on a pipe (3.2.332–60). When he, in a farcical gag, pressed the pipe to his bottom, shrill sounds of a piccolo, bass, and drum mocked at a simple-minded proletarian song celebrating the victory of the Soviet troops over the Chinese in 1929.[4]

The question for us now is how far the whole production went in its satirical reflection of the Soviet political scene. Since Lenin's death in 1924, a merciless fight for the post of general secretary of the Soviet Communist Party had been raging, and Stalin was getting rid of his rivals with Machiavellian deception and Tamerlanian ruthlessness. Almost unavoidably, Akimov's grotesque production was attacked by Communist critics and soon removed from the repertoire despite the fact that crowds of Muscovites were spending hours in ticket lines to see it and one New York critic called it 'the best show in Europe'.

Then, however, something entirely unexpected happened: Akimov moved the production to Leningrad. The transfer was formally based on a previous contract but there can be little doubt that it must have been approved by the highest Communist authorities of the city and region of Leningrad. If we remember that the post of the Leningrad party secretary was held by Stalin's chief rival of the early 1930s, Sergei Kirov, astonishing associations and parallels emerge. The increasingly popular Kirov was assassinated in Leningrad in 1934 in a most mysterious conspiracy which has never been fully uncovered, as it was probably instigated by Stalin himself, determined to stifle the growing opposition by unleashing an unprecedented purge of all his possible rivals and enemies. When Stalin arrived in Leningrad in December 1934 to kiss dear comrade Kirov in the coffin, the paradoxes of Soviet reality reached one of their climaxes.

With subtle insight, Akimov's *Hamlet* anticipated both the grotesque and the tragic features of Stalin's monstrous show, including his imitation of Claudius' hypocritical regret at his 'dear brother's death' (*Hamlet*, 1.2.17 and 19). The production closed with a scathingly ironic quotation from the German humanist and reformer Ulrich von Hutten whose lines were inserted into the text as a leitmotiv and were repeated, in an abridged version, by Horatio as the last line of the play:

'Oh what a joy it is to be alive!'

Another memorable production was *King Lear* at the State Jewish Theatre (GOSET) in Moscow. The theatre, known in Yiddish as Melucha, was founded in Leningrad in 1919 but soon moved to Moscow, producing mostly modern plays. Premièred in 1935, the Yiddish *King Lear* was directed by Sergei Radlov, and the title role was played by the leading actor and manager of the company, Solomon Mikhoels (1890–1948). His performance was called simply but beautifully a 'song' by Gordon Craig, while a Russian scholar, directing attention to his intellectual capacities, characterized him as an actor-philosopher.

Short and fragile in stature, Mikhoels decided not to wear a beard, in defiance of the customary huge beards of Russian rulers. He needed his full face to express all the drastic changes of Lear's mind and feelings. In the opening of the play, he strutted as the all-powerful master of his kingdom, dividing it, in a kind of philosophic experiment, to prove that even without his kingly attributes he would remain the centre of the world. When his illusion was subjected to a radical exposure culminating, symbolically, in the storm, he started to perceive the 'double face' of reality, as Mikhoels himself put it: not only its deformity and brutality but also its beauty, in the person of Cordelia. As he was conducted to prison together with his true and beloved daughter, he grew into a man who had gained real wisdom and inner freedom:

Come, let's away to prison.
We two alone will sing like birds i'th' cage. (*King Lear*, 5.3.8–9)

Another Russian critic described the production in both historical and topical terms:

The stage of the State Jewish Theatre is full of the breath of a horrible age, the breath of legalized betrayals, legalized murders, legalized robberies, legalized brutalities, legalized war of everybody against everybody... But at the same time we also feel the breath of a new age, an age in which the voices of humanity are raised, grow stronger, and sound louder.[5]

The Jewish *King Lear* continued to offer wisdom and consolation throughout the horrible Stalinist trials and Gulag imprisonments as well as the whole of the Second World War during which the Nazis were operating their gas chambers in the concentration camps to exterminate, in their gruesomely systematic way, 'impure' and 'inferior' races: Jews, Slavs, Gypsies. When the German armies were penetrating close to Moscow, the Jewish Theatre was evacuated to Tashkent in far-off Uzbekistan with *King Lear* as its highlight.

In 1941 another *King Lear* opened in Leningrad, and was to survive the whole war. Directed by Grigori Kozintsev (1905–73) with music by Dmitri Shostakovich, it continued to haunt Kozintsev's imagination until he could film it in 1967–70 (see next chapter). In 1943–4, Kozintsev directed *Othello* for the Leningrad Pushkin Theatre; by that time, the theatre had had to be evacuated to Novosibirsk in south Siberia. There are brief records of more productions of Shakespeare's plays during the war in other Soviet towns and different languages.

A rich source of relief and pleasure was found in Shakespeare's comedies. An unusually successful production of *The Taming of the Shrew* started at the Red Army Theatre in Moscow in 1938 and continued to be applauded, through the whole war, by both soldiers and civilians, in spite, or rather because, of their terrible suffering (their total losses reached the almost unbelievable number of 20–30 million). The director, Alexei Popov (1892–1961), a follower of Stanislavsky, was intent on stressing Shakespeare's humanism, which transformed the old theme of brutal taming into a much more subtle comedy of love.

The Moscow Katherine and Petruccio fell in love with each other at first sight, so that their conventional fight between a shrew and a fortune-hunter was changed into an exciting love game between two equally proud and intelligent young people who tamed each other but also themselves. The most difficult stumbling-block to this interpretation was Katherine's final notorious speech about the unconditional subjection of wives to husbands. With her quick wit, Katherine had an inkling that Petruccio had placed a bet on her obedience and she was ready to win him his wager but, at the same time, trusted him to remain faithful to their mutual love as the best foundation of their happiness.

A special feature of the staging was three big horses built of papier mâché from carousel models and centred on a pivot that moved up and down, giving the impression that Petruccio, Kate, and Hortensio, who were riding them, were returning from Petruccio's country house to Padua (4.6). This scene, developed from popular entertainment, was among the most applauded attractions of the whole production.

The greatest miracle of Shakespearian inspiration at that 'fearful'st time' (*Richard III*, 3.4.104) was created by Sergei Prokofiev (1891–1953), composer, conductor, and pianist, who became a wandering star in 1918 and returned to his homeland in the 1930s (Soviet sources give the year of his definite return as 1932, whereas Western dating is 1936 or even 1938). In 1935, Prokofiev finished the first version of his ballet *Romeo and Juliet* and submitted it to the Bolshoi (Large) Theatre in Moscow. Characteristically for the unpredictable situation in the Soviet Union, the score was turned down, so that the world première of the ballet had to take place in democratic and avant-garde Czechoslovakia (in Brno, the capital of Moravia) in 1938. Meanwhile, Prokofiev kept reworking the score and, moreover, adapting it into orchestral suites for concert halls. Only in 1940 was *Romeo and Juliet* performed in Leningrad at the Kirov Theatre, the part of Juliet being danced by Galina Ulanova, a ravishing representative of the great school of Russian ballet. At long last, in 1946, Prokofiev's Shakespearian masterpiece, with Ulanova as its chief star, made a conquest of Moscow, when the Bolshoi Theatre, in an act of expiation, provided for a most spectacular staging.

The whole structure of the ballet was built on contrasts between the expanse of chorus scenes on the square or in the ballroom and the intimacy of Juliet's bedroom, Friar Laurence's cell, or, finally, Juliet's tomb (the most famous scene of Shakespeare's tragedy, Juliet's balcony, was of course not so good for dancing). These contrasts in structure were developed to bring out the main dramatic conflict between warlike violence, old authority, and conventional morals on the one hand and, on the other, youthful love and yearning for peace. Juliet grew from an inexperienced, perplexed girl into a sublime heroine, faithful to her lover and her ideal of love. The final image of her death was unforgettable: instead of following Shakespeare's text and stabbing herself with Romeo's dagger, she slowly drank Romeo's poison from his lips and died with a gesture of final victory. A strong effect of catharsis sprang from the suggestion that the individual fates of the lovers were transcended by the invincibility of their ideal of love and life in peace.

Prokofiev's score survives as an inexhaustible source of both ballet and concert interpretations. In comparison with Tchaikovsky's fantasy overture on the same theme, it is distinctly modernistic in sound and rhythm but, at the same time, movingly lyrical and transparent, with only occasional touches of Prokofiev's earlier harsh and strident style. Economic in the use of instruments, it reduces the fury of sound in favour of subtlety, tenderness, and depth of feeling. The breath of youthful life and love permeates the whole composition and although it is stifled in the final catastrophe, it reverberates in us as an experience of lasting value.

The unpredictable wilfulness of the Stalinist regime marked the entrances and mysterious exits of one of the most active and versatile Shakespearian directors of the Soviet era, Sergei Radlov (1892–1958), whose name is a rare item in Soviet theatre histories and encyclopedias. He started his career by organizing and directing the first company to entertain Bolshevik military units fighting in the Civil War. He was also responsible for mass pageants and other festivities celebrating the October Revolution. In the 1920s, he experimented in expressionist productions, including *The Merry Wives of Windsor* (1920) and *Othello* (1927); in the 1930s he more or less conformed to the official line of socialist realism but continued to direct productions of remarkable psychological insight, especially the two Moscow Shakespeares discussed above: *Othello* at the Maly Theatre and *King Lear* at the State Jewish Theatre. His Leningrad productions of *Othello* (1932, 1935) and *Romeo and Juliet* (1934) were followed by *Hamlet* (1938) with incidental music by Prokofiev. All the three tragedies were performed in one cycle during the Leningrad Shakespeare Festival organized by Radlov in 1939 and accompanied by a volume of essays entitled *Shakespeare 1564–1939* (Leningrad, 1939). The production of *Romeo and Juliet* was outshone in the following year by Prokofiev's ballet, in which Radlov participated as co-author of the libretto and co-director.

During the German blockade of Leningrad, Radlov's theatrical troupe was evacuated to the northern Caucasus with Shakespeare as part and parcel of their repertoire. More and more, the Radlov Men were being embroiled in the colossal chaos of the Second World War and their lives were becoming unbelievably adventurous. According to available testimony, they were made prisoners of war and transported to Germany at the end of 1942, but their principal was able to persuade some of the more enlightened German officers to allow him and his men to perform for Russian prisoners of war working in German factories and for soldiers of General Vlasov, who commanded a Russian-Ukrainian army fighting on the side of the Germans. In 1944, the Radlov Men got as far as the occupied part of France, escaped to Switzerland, and finally arranged to be flown to London.[6] Radlov's career became a very special case of a wandering star during the Second World War, but his further fate cannot be described other than as that of a lost star. Probably he decided to leave England and return home, only to be treated like other prisoners of war and sent to one of the innumerable Stalinist labour camps. Alternatively, he could have been allowed to work at some insignificant post as a non-person.

Soon after Stalin's death, Radlov resurfaced and, according to a Soviet theatre encyclopedia, worked as director again until his death in 1958. He did not live long enough to be called back to Leningrad or Moscow so that he closed his theatrical career in the Latvian town of Daugavpils and then in Riga, the capital of Latvia. The available data inform us that he produced *Hamlet* with Prokofiev's music in Daugavpils in 1954 and *King Lear* with Shostakovich's music in Riga at the end of the same year; both productions were in Russian. It is not for us to pass judgement on Radlov's extremely chequered career. All we can say is that his last two recorded productions in Latvia should be considered as acts of artistic resilience and perseverance.

II

Although the Baltic republic of Latvia was absorbed into the Soviet Empire in 1940, occupied by Nazi Germany in 1941, and returned to the Soviet Union in 1944, it enjoyed a brief period of independence and democracy between the two wars. The old international sea-port of Riga, which had been visited by English strolling players as early as 1644 and 1647–8, saw an unprecedented series of Shakespeare's comedies and tragedies in Latvian in the heady years of independence. When the democratic regime was overthrown by an autocratic *coup d'état* in 1934, a Latvian *Julius Caesar* was staged in Riga, presenting an unflattering portrait and the fall of the dictator. The highest circles of the new government concluded that the production was inappropriate and ordered it to be removed from the repertoire. The director, Eduards Smiļģis, was accused of sympathies with the Soviet Union and, personally, with the actor Michael Chekhov, who was active in Riga for about two years before the autocratic takeover but, as we know, was definitely not a supporter of the Soviets. Getting short shrift, Smiļģis was replaced by a compliant director. After appropriate adaptations, *Julius Caesar* was rerun and shown to Sir Archibald Flower, the Stratford patron of the Shakespeare Memorial Theatre, who was invited to read a paper at the University of Riga on 'Shakespeare's Significance in our Day'.[7]

In those years of growing economic and political crisis, *Julius Caesar* was attracting heightened attention in both the East and the West. Orson Welles's much-discussed New York production in 1937 was preceded by two perhaps more remarkable stagings in Eastern Europe. In 1928, six years before the Latvian staging, *Julius Caesar* was produced in Poland, which was also liberated after the First World War and enjoyed a brief period of democracy followed by a *coup d'état* (1926), in which Marshal Józef Piłsudski, who had fought victoriously against the Red Army in 1919–20, assumed political power to rule the country by veiled military dictatorship. In a coded message about the danger of dictatorship, Leon Schiller directed *Julius Caesar* in Warsaw, presenting the title hero as a strongly ambivalent aristocrat who deserved to be both admired and hated. Possibly following the Moscow MAT *Julius Caesar* of 1903, Schiller accentuated the mass scenes, 'the game of the crowd', as he called them, suggesting that the people could be manipulated by cunning politicians in a game of power politics. The ominous storm before Caesar's assassination was displayed in an interpolated scene, expressing the fusion of natural and social forces by intensified lighting and mass pantomime. The final battle scenes were enacted on a bare stage with nothing but Cubist rocks and a large cyclorama in the background, on which the white lances of the soldiers were reflected as dark shadows. The battle at Philippi was projected into the future to recall both the early Renaissance battle paintings by Uccello and the recent actual battle of Riga in which Pilsudski's army had scored a victory.

Leon Schiller's *Julius Caesar* has by now been recognized in the West too, being praised for 'the masterful combination of lighting, projections, actors, levels, and props' which 'gave the audience one of the most memorable sights of Shakespeare in the century'.[8] Considering the possible influence of the MAT production, we should add that Leon Schiller was a practical follower of two very original artists and thinkers: Gordon Craig, whose collaboration with the MAT has been noticed, and Stanisław Wyspiański (1868–1907), a Polish symbolist painter, poet, playwright, designer, and director whom Craig considered a uniquely complete man of the theatre. As a neo-Romantic visionary, Wyspiański had anticipated some of Craig's daring ideas. He saw *Hamlet* as an incessant process of searching for truth and called for an 'immense theatre' in which word and action would combine with visual effects in a great spectacle of liberation, both individual and national. This is exactly what Schiller achieved in his overpowering *Julius Caesar*.

The second memorable production of the tragedy in East Central Europe took place in 1936 in Czechoslovakia, which also won its independence in 1918, after 300 years of subjection to the Habsburg Empire. In contrast to the Fascist tendencies in Poland or Hungary, the new Czechoslovak Republic, uniting the historical lands of Bohemia, Moravia, and Slovakia, was able to preserve democracy until it was destroyed by Hitler, and his fanatical German supporters within the republic, in 1938–9. Its capital Prague was characterized by a symbiosis of Slavonic, German, and Jewish culture (e.g. Franz Kafka) and offered asylum to refugees from both Communist Russia (a Prague group of the MAT was active from 1923 to the early 1930s) and Nazi Germany (briefly to Max Reinhardt, Bertolt Brecht, Thomas Mann, etc.). The Czech National Theatre in Prague carried out its revivalist mission and, emulating the Shakespeare Jubilee of 1864, commemorated the 300th anniversary of the poet's death in 1916 by performing fifteen of his plays in an enthusiastically received cycle which aimed at proving that the Czechs had reached cultural maturity and deserved political independence as well.

After the liberation in 1918, the Prague National Theatre continued to give Shakespeare pride of place in innovative productions inspired mainly by Stanislavsky's MAT as well as German expressionist staging, especially by Max Reinhardt and Leopold Jessner. The production of *Julius Caesar* in 1936 was directed by Jiří Frejka (1902–52), who followed Shakespeare's text quite faithfully in all its ambiguities, calling attention to the precarious position of the republicans threatened by both dictatorial usurpation of power and the revolt of the masses incited by demagogues. Although the relevance of the production to the contemporary situation in Europe was in the air, there was no attempt at a direct political statement. Instead, Frejka wanted, according to his own words, to give full voice to Shakespeare's art of creating archetypal political characters and conflicts.

A more straightforward appeal to audiences was made by the scenic metaphors of the designer František Tröster, with whom the tendency toward the massive in Gordon Craig, the MAT, and the expressionists reached hyperbolic proportions. In the opening scenes, a steeply tilted pedestal, looking as if it would fall down at any minute, was surmounted by the legs of a colossal equestrian statue extending high up out of sight, suggesting that the megalomania of Caesar was deformed by both Mussolini and Hitler out of all proportion. When Caesar appeared at the Capitol, the set was changed into an upright pedestal on which a titanic head of the Emperor was towering. After Caesar's assassination, the whole set collapsed, and the colossal head split open on the floor, which was littered with surrealist broken columns. The pillars of dictatorship were shown to be as vulnerable as the dictator himself, exposed as a colossus of clay.

Tröster's scenographic 'hyperbolic realism', as it was called, was applied in the following year to a completely different play: the Czech National's *As You Like It*, in which the Forest of Arden was represented by giant stylized maple and alder leaves and their projections on a cyclorama. This scenographic device anticipated some Western sets for *As You Like It* in the 1960s and later, when huge leaves and giant trees became all the fashion, extending from Stratford-upon-Avon as far as Canada or Germany and Norway.

Much greater liberties with Shakespeare's text were taken by the director, composer, playwright, and theatre theoretician E. F. Burian (1904–59) in his avant-garde Prague theatre. A friend of Bertolt Brecht and creator of a lyric counterpart to Brecht's epic theatre, Burian first tackled Shakespeare in strongly adapted and updated versions of *The Merchant of Venice* (1934) and *Hamlet* (1936). As in other democratic countries, the 1930s were marked in Czechoslovakia by the growing influence of the Communists not only among the workers but also among the intelligentsia and the artists. Although Burian did not subscribe to the official Soviet line of socialist realism, preferring his own poetic staging, he was arrested as a Communist in 1941 by the Gestapo and held in two concentration camps. Immediately after his return to Prague in 1945, he felt an irrepressible urge to free himself from the inhuman experience by realizing his vision of *Romeo and Juliet*. He remembered acutely that his longings in the concentration camps tended to take on the shape of women in different plays produced by himself or other directors. For him, *Romeo and Juliet* was 'an unfulfilled desire ending in death', 'an unfulfilled desire to live a little like human beings, unfulfilled because two houses were in strife'.[9]

Following Shakespeare's text more faithfully than in the pre-war adaptations, he presented the whole action as a dream of a concentration camp prisoner, a dream of free life and passionate love, shattered by violent, brutal reality. The production opened with a nightmarish scene of a concentration camp at night, showing a watch-tower with a revolving machine gun and a searchlight intermittently flooding the *Appel-platz*, the Nazi roll-call square fenced with barbed wire. In a dark cell in the corner, poorly lit by a bare bulb, a starved and manhandled prisoner breathed out Romeo's lines of desire for Juliet. Suddenly, his feverish dream came true, and Juliet soared 'aloft' as a 'bright angel', transforming the monstrous watch-tower into her balcony. When Mercutio and Benvolio appeared, the prisoner could not resist joining them as Romeo with a blood-red triangle on his breast, even though his Craigian dream was still disturbed by recurrent scenographic evocations of the Nazi hell. More and more, however, those intrusions served as a gruesome foil for the sonorous beauty of Shakespeare's most lyrical tragedy, especially in the lines of Juliet who grew into a symbol of love overcoming the horrors of any time or place.

The breakdown of the Austro-Hungarian monarchy brought to life new artistic developments not only in such newly formed states as Latvia, Poland, Czechoslovakia, or Yugoslavia but also in Austria itself and especially in Vienna, the former capital of the Habsburg Empire. The imperial Court Theatre was transformed into a modern republican Federal Theatre (Bundestheater) where Richard Strauss was active as managing director of the Opera. Drama continued to be played in the Burgtheater, which had moved to a new building opposite the Town Hall in 1888, was destroyed in 1945, and rebuilt in 1955. In the years 1920–38, a long Shakespearian series was produced there, amounting to twenty-two plays, some staying in the repertoire for more than a decade (such as *Hamlet* or *Coriolanus*), others introduced twice during the period (*Macbeth, Much Ado About Nothing, Antony and Cleopatra, The Winter's Tale, Richard II, Romeo and Juliet, Julius Caesar*). In the off-centre Josefstädter Theater, Max Reinhardt produced seven Shakespeare plays between 1924 and 1938, until he had to emigrate to America. Among them was his great favourite *A Midsummer Night's Dream* (1925), which he staged numerous times between 1905 and 1939 in cities as far apart as Berlin, Budapest, Florence, Oxford, Stockholm, and Los Angeles and which he filmed in Hollywood in 1935.

An innovative director, translator, playwright, theatre critic, and theoretician, Sándor Hevesi (1873–1939), was appointed managing director of the Hungarian National Theatre in Budapest in 1922. He was a friend and correspondent of Gordon Craig, Max Reinhardt, Granville-Barker, G. B. Shaw, and many other theatre people all over Europe. In his search for a 'real Shakespeare', as close as possible to the simplicity of the Elizabethan stage, Hevesi radically reduced the elaborate pictorial scenography surviving from the nineteenth century. His enormous energy and dedication resulted in several Shakespeare cycles and many more productions of individual plays: at times, as many as eighteen were in his repertoire. During the growing Fascist pressures in Hungary, he had to leave the National Theatre in 1932 on charges of disregard for commercial success. This was a false accusation; Hevesi declared in so many words that Shakespeare paid like no other foreign playwright, being the National's 'best-seller'.[10] Hevesi's contribution to the modern development of Shakespearian production and interpretation was recognized internationally in his own time and has been fully appreciated since the end of the Second World War in his native country too. Nowadays, he is considered to be the chief representative of the first golden age of the Hungarian National Theatre.

FURTHER READING

The best information on Russian émigré theatre in the years 1905–40 is in Laurence Senelick (ed.), *Wandering Stars* (Iowa City, 1992). Eleanor Rowe's monograph *Hamlet: A Window on Russia* (New York, 1976), recommended for Chapter 3, is equally valid for the periods after the Bolshevik Revolution and after the Second World War. The same is true for the volume of essays recommended for Chapter 4: *Shakespeare in Hungary*, edited by Holgar Klein and Péter Dávidházi (Lewiston, NY, 1996). Of the Soviet publications, a few are in English: Mikhail M. Morozov, *Shakespeare on the Soviet Stage* (London, 1947); *Shakespeare in the Soviet Union*, compiled by Roman Samarin and Alexander Nikolyukin (Moscow, 1966). The latter presents badly reproduced but mostly fascinating photographs of Russian, Georgian, Armenian, Jewish, north Ossetic, and Estonian Shakespeare productions. Even more fascinating are the illustrations in Dennis Kennedy's excellent *Looking at Shakespeare: A Visual History of Twentieth-Century Performance* (Cambridge, 1993), which includes the work of some important directors and designers from East Central Europe.

5

Shakespeare behind the Iron Curtain

I

The sweeping victories of the Soviet Army and Western Allies over Hitler's last resistance in 1945 were greeted with enthusiasm all over Eastern Europe. It was not long, however, before it was apparent that Stalin had decided to enlarge and buttress his empire by dictatorial methods. Except for Austria, which managed to achieve neutrality, all East European countries, including East Germany (from 1949 called officially the German Democratic Republic), were turned successively into totalitarian states in which the Communist parties assumed all the decisive power. As early as 1946, Winston Churchill sounded an emotional note of warning in his talk at Westminster College, Fulton (Missouri).

With his experience as an old British imperialist, he could well imagine what the new Soviet imperialism, based on the ruthless methods of tsarist expansionism, had in store. Acknowledging his admiration and respect for the Soviet people and, personally, his wartime friend Stalin, Churchill mobilized the West against the danger of the 'Iron Curtain' which was being dropped across the European continent, preventing citizens of the new Soviet bloc from moving and acting freely. Churchill's theatrical metaphor soon came into common use because it signified the split among the war Allies, resulting in two huge military formations which were to oppose each other in a Cold War: the North Atlantic Treaty Organization (NATO) and the Warsaw Pact. Although the latter was formally signed only in 1955, it was based on Stalin's foreign policy, confronting Western capitalism with the atomic military power of the Soviet Union, supported by the satellite states of Poland, East Germany, Czechoslovakia, Hungary, Romania, Bulgaria, and Albania.

How did Shakespeare fare inside the Communist bloc? Generally, he was tolerated and even generously subsidized by Communist authorities but, at the same time, strictly controlled. Soon after the war, many new professional and amateur theatres were opened all over the bloc and theatre arts schools with university status were founded with the idea of educating new socialist actors and directors who would go on inspiring the masses in the spirit of socialism. Of all playwrights, Shakespeare was the most attractive for theatres, schools, and research institutes because he represented the highest artistic value approved by Marx and Engels themselves. Even the dyed-in-the-wool apparatchiks did not dare to attack him openly, although they found it personally offensive to hear from Hamlet that something was rotten in the state of Denmark. They had to admit that Shakespeare was an ideal classic to reach the widest strata of readers and audiences and thus to bridge the gap which had frequently developed between modern art and the people. The popular, realistic, and humanistic character of Shakespeare's plays was discussed thoroughly, often more profusely than profoundly but sometimes revealingly, especially in books and essays by A. A. Smirnov, M. M. Morozov, György Lukácz, A. A. Anikst, and Robert Weimann.

Despite the pressure exerted by militant Communist critics who leaned over backward to enlist Shakespeare in their campaign against Western capitalism and abused all those who were not ready to join them in what they called the fight for peace, some traditional scholars continued their research, often in very difficult conditions. The best examples are the Bulgarian professor Marco Mincoff, whose publications on Shakespeare and Elizabethan drama won him international recognition that had to be respected even at home, or the Czech scholar Otakar Vočadlo, who returned from the Nazi concentration camp at Buchenwald to resume his classes at Charles University in Prague but was pensioned by totalitarian authorities after 1948; never despairing, he started to prepare a scholarly edition of *The Complete Works of Shakespeare* in classical Czech translations which was finally published with his prefaces and richly informative commentaries in six volumes between 1959 and 1964. In the Soviet Union itself, teacher and scholar Leonid Pinsky survived five years in a Stalinist concentration camp in the early 1950s to produce original books on the art of the Renaissance (1961) and Shakespeare (1971) which exercised influence among both serious students and innovative artists, such as the film-maker Grigori Kozintsev.

Whereas Pinsky has remained practically unknown in the West, the poet, novelist, and translator Boris Pasternak (1890–1960) was awarded the Nobel Prize in 1958 but had to decline it, as he was exposed to unrelenting harassment from Communist bureaucracy. Pasternak was attached to Shakespeare for all his creative life. In his best early verse collection *My Sister Life* (pub. 1922), the poem 'English Lessons' featured Desdemona and Ophelia 'letting their passions slip from their shoulders like old rags' and entering 'into the reservoir of the universe'; the novel *Doctor Zhivago* (pub. first in Italy, 1957) con-cluded with a sequence of poems headed by 'Hamlet' who bore an unmistakable resemblance to both Zhivago and Pasternak himself:

> I stand alone. All else is swamped by Pharisaism.
> To live life to the end is not a childish task.

In the 1930s, Pasternak gave up his attempts to join the ranks of disciplined followers of socialist realism and started his 'long silent duel' with the dictator. Paradoxically, Stalin himself showed respect for Pasternak's integrity and tamed the bloodthirsty pursuers of the poet by a surprising command: Do not touch this cloud-dweller!

Escaping into translation, Pasternak turned his creative energy to producing genuine Russian versions of Goethe's *Faust* and selected poems of Ralegh, Jonson, Shelley, Byron, and Keats. Shakespeare, however, remained his chief concern, and translations of *Hamlet*, *Romeo and Juliet*, *Antony and Cleopatra*, *Othello*, *1* and *2 Henry IV*, *King Lear*, *Macbeth*, and selected sonnets became his great passion and consolation before, during, and after the Second World War. Among all of them, *Hamlet* proved to be the most essential, as it allowed him to vent his own painful feelings and ruminations about himself and his time. In the early version of the soliloquy 'To be or not to be', he castigated 'the onslaughts of pursuers', 'the red tape', 'foul-mouth petty officials, and the kicks of the worthless, kicking the worthy'. Although in his later versions he toned down his radical images, he definitely retained his original interpretation of Hamlet's character and of the whole tragedy. In his vision, *Hamlet* was first and foremost a tragedy of duty and self-denial, 'a drama of high calling, of a pre-ordained heroic death, of entrusted destiny'. The destiny and duty consisted not so much in the role of an avenger as in that of 'a judge of his own time and servant of the future'.[1] It is not difficult to see that this was essentially what Pasternak himself was striving after to the end of his life.

Although Pasternak's *Hamlet* was judged by some critics and scholars to be shaped too much in his own image of great seriousness, showing little sense of Hamlet's mocking and sarcastic wit, it was warmly accepted by the film and theatre director Grigori Kozintsev, who decided to stage the tragedy in Leningrad immediately after Stalin's death. In his letter to Pasternak, Kozintsev wrote by the end of 1953: 'Prosy word-for-word translations should not be made, the philosophic-psychological structure is inseparable from the poetic.' He praised Pasternak for the fluency and transparency of his blank verse and did not blame him for reducing Shakespeare's metaphoric exuberance to a more sober imagery.

The only difference between the director and the translator arose when they discussed the ending of the tragedy. Whereas Kozintsev did not like the final 'operatic' appearance of Fortinbras, traditionally presented with 'a feather on his helmet, banners, fanfares, a crowd of extras', Pasternak wrote that the ending seemed 'natural' to him, as it was 'the roar of life's general continuation after the silence of isolated death'. Finally, he complied with Kozintsev's view and translated Shakespeare's Sonnet 74 with which the Leningrad production closed, stressing 'the force of poetry which refuses to make peace with the baseness and degradation of the era' and which 'will outlive the emblems of potentates and the thrones of Tsars'.[2] Oblique as it had to be even in a private letter, Kozintsev's view implied a resolute condemnation of the dead dictator who had been chiefly responsible for imposing the worst methods of tsarist tyranny on the Soviet Union and its satellites.

During 1954, a periodic *Hamlet* fever gripped Russian theatres, the more intense in that it broke out after a long-term veto on the play by Stalin. As the prisoners were returning from the Gulag Archipelago, proving that the worst days of Stalin's terror were over, Hamlet's questions about the meaning of man's existence and action were revived with most painful insistence.

Besides Kozintsev's Leningrad *Hamlet*, most attention was attracted by the production of the tragedy in Moscow. Directed by Nikolai Okhlopkov, it became well known as the 'Iron Curtain *Hamlet*' because its central scenic metaphor was a massive pair of metal gates that could slide forward and back or could swing partially or fully apart in the centre. They were divided into rectangular cells suggesting prison bars. In the play-within-the-play of the strolling actors, the individual cells were transformed into theatre boxes so that the court was watching the performance from above. When Laertes returned suddenly to avenge his father's death, a second iron grille was lowered to prevent the angry populace from breaking into the palace. Prince Hamlet was a youth of a loving nature, whose feelings and ideals had been violated. Suddenly discovering the truth about his family and his society, he reacted with the bitter irony or even fury of a grossly deceived citizen. Although young Muscovites greeted their fellow student and the whole production with stormy applause, it was not allowed to continue for long. Perhaps by way of compensation, Peter Brook was invited to visit Moscow with his *Hamlet*, starring Paul Scofield, by the end of 1955. It was the first English company to appear in Russia since 1917.

II

The most overtly oppositional *Hamlet* in the whole Warsaw Pact bloc was produced in Cracow in 1956, right after the 20th Congress of the Soviet Communist Party, at which the first secretary Nikita Khrushchev made his far-reaching revelations about Stalin's atrocities. The director Roman Zawistowski cut the text into a clear and sharp version, concentrated practically on one issue: politics. The production was full of pain and hatred against Stalinist oppression and surveillance. 'Watch', 'enquire', and 'prison' were the words most insistently addressed at the audience. Prince Hamlet was a young, charismatic rebel, 'rid of illusion, sarcastic, passionate and brutal', 'wild and drunk with indignation'.[3] The simplification of his character and of the whole play made it frighteningly straightforward and effective. At Elsinore, every curtain was hiding a spy, everything was corroded by suspicion and fear. Hamlet feigned madness in order to deceive the tyrant and to show that politics itself was madness, when it was destroying all feelings of love and friendship. Above all, the mask of madness served him to brace himself for the decisive fight with the oppressor. His wit and bravery were rewarded by a magnificent funeral: his body was carried high by Fortinbras's captains in reverence of the hero whose death was not a defeat.

It was not by chance that the Cracow production was chosen, out of many Polish *Hamlets* produced after the Second World War, as the basis for the discussion of the tragedy in Jan Kott's phenomenally successful and influential *Shakespeare our Contemporary* (first published in Polish as *Sketches on Shakespeare*, 1961, in French 1962, in English separately in London and New York, 1964). As Kott (born 1914) was at that time professor of literature and drama at the University of Warsaw, his essays grew out of his fascination with some Polish Shakespearian productions and also with Peter Brook's *Titus Andronicus* which, in a revival for a continental tour, was introduced to Warsaw in 1957 as a perfectly stylized specimen of the theatre of cruelty. Kott's approach to Shakespeare as a man of the theatre, whose plays were exceptionally suitable for contemporary stage and film, was hailed by many actors and directors as the most stimulating book of drama criticism of the period. In a preface to the English edition, Peter Brook praised Kott as unique, learned, informed, serious, precise, and scholarly 'without what we associate with scholarship'. Unique Kott certainly was but not precise or scholarly in any sense of the word. His essays were marked by a number of elementary mistakes and misreadings which provoked one distinguished scholar to call them 'The Shakespearian Rag'.[4]

Although Brook and Kott spoke condescendingly about 'learned Shakespearian scholars' whose pedantic research behind ivy-covered walls was bound to offer 'ridiculous and childish results', Kott's own statements amounted sometimes to howlers. For instance, he wrote about *Sir Thomas More* as 'a lost tragedy', whereas its preserved manuscript has been edited and discussed intensively by several generations of scholars. More serious than individual inaccuracies were Kott's sweeping generalizations, such as the one concerning Shakespeare's early and middle plays: 'Of all the important works written by Shakespeare before 1600, i.e. what nineteenth-century scholars called his optimistic period, only *Henry IV* can be called a cheerful play.'[5] Unless we are aiming at originality at all costs, we are obliged to stand by those scorned literary historians, for the majority of the plays of this period are indeed cheerful, although Shakespeare introduces dark figures, sharp conflicts, or the theme of death even into his comedies.

While we can understand Kott's overstated view that the harmony and idyll of the Forest of Arden in *As You Like It* is 'split' by Jacques's bitter mockery, we can hardly believe that in the hot dream of a midsummer night Titania literally passes 'through the dark sphere of animal love' and frees herself from inhibitions by raping poor Bottom transformed into an enormously virile monstrous ass. Yet even if we grant Titania and the young lovers their Kottian orgy, we still have to restate that Shakespeare's early and middle comedies are not primarily cruel, brutal, terrifying, abhorrent, and scatological but essentially cheerful, festive, and, yes, optimistic. Their complexity, of course, cannot be fully appreciated if we see them simply in terms of the binary opposites of either optimism or cruelty.

The most ambitious of Kott's theories was his interpretation of Shakespeare's conception of history as a 'Grand Mechanism', cruel and absurd, crushing all attempts at individual freedom of action. In his long introductory essay 'On Kings', he connected this concept with a 'grand staircase' on which there treads a constant procession of rulers who reach the top only to be hurled into the abyss. For all its apparent originality, the image of the Grand Mechanism did nothing more than brush up, in fashionable terms, the medieval concept of the Wheel of Fortune carrying ambitious magistrates to the highest point and then dragging them down to finish the full circle. Naturally, we find in Shakespeare dramatic and poetic elaborations of old ideological patterns. More important, however, are his new dynamic ideas and images, of which perhaps the most remarkable are some aspects of Time which bring movement and tension into both individual lives and history as a whole.

Although Kott could write engrossingly about Time when he discussed the *Sonnets* and *Troilus and Cressida*, he narrowed his metaphor of the Grand Mechanism to a rigid formula: 'For there are no bad kings, or good kings; kings are only kings. Or let us put it in modern terms: there is only the king's situation, and the system. This situation leaves no room for freedom of choice.' Against this one must state that one of Shakespeare's greatest achievements was to create strongly individualized characters who were not willing, even in moments of great crisis or catastrophe, to give up their individuality and personal responsibility. It is perhaps enough to recall Richard II's penitent recognition of the causes of his fall:

> I wasted time, and now doth time waste me. (*Richard II*, 5.5.49)

One can appreciate Kott's disillusioned view of history as a nightmare associated with his native country's and his own experience during the Second World War and its Stalinist aftermath. His illumination of the darkest corners of Shakespeare's histories was a salutary antidote to the overtly patriotic or imperialistic interpretations of such plays as *Henry V* or *King John*. But in supporting his arguments Kott used quotations from Shakespeare arbitrarily, cutting lines or whole passages that did not suit his interpretation. Towards the end of his essay on kings, he quoted the famous line repeated desperately by Richard III on Bosworth field:

> A horse! A horse! My kingdom for a horse! (*Richard III*, 5.7.7, 13)

Kott's comment was magisterial but utterly misleading: 'So, this is how much all his efforts have been worth. This is the real price of power, of history, of the crown adorning the Lord's Anointed. One good horse is worth more than the entire kingdom. This is the last sentence of the great cycle of Shakespeare's historical plays.'

It cannot in any sense be said that Richard's cry is the last sentence of Shakespeare's historical plays, although one can imagine a production of *Richard III* ending impressively with Richard's exclamation. A full critical analysis should not disregard the final patriotic speech by Richmond (Henry VII) who curses the dead tyrant and glorifies the renewal of peace and unity in England after the madness of civil war. Nor should one ignore the fact that *Richard III* was followed by six more English histories. Even if we arrange them not in the order in which they were probably written but according to historical chronology, we still are left with *Henry VIII*, which was included in the First Folio at the end of the section of Histories and is considered by modern editors to be written entirely by Shakespeare or in substantial cooperation with John Fletcher (Kott dismisses it as 'Fletcher's tragedy' with only a few scenes by Shakespeare). We cannot brush this play aside simply because it does not fit our theory.

If there is an overall vision in Shakespeare's English histories, then it penetrates through all the horrors and bloodshed of the Wars of the Roses to England's unification and prosperity under the new dynasty of the Tudors. More original and exciting, however, are Shakespeare's dramatic insights into the greatly different minds of the individual English rulers and their intricate relations with the immense variety of their subjects, both high and low, tragic and comic, patriotic and subversive.

Even in his best essay, 'King Lear or Endgame', Kott did not avoid simplifications and omissions. He managed to discuss the tragedy without mentioning Cordelia by name (he only referred to 'one good daughter' from 'a nursery tale'), which is about as eccentric as discussing *Othello* without mentioning Desdemona. Cordelia simply did not suit Kott's vision of *King Lear* as a great predecessor of the contemporary theatre of cruelty and tragic grotesque. What he said about Lear, the Fool, Gloucester, and Poor Tom, however, was mostly brilliant and thrilling. The idea of comparing *King Lear* with the drama of the absurd, and particularly with Beckett's *Endgame* and *Waiting for Godot*, threw a new light on many scenes of the tragedy and, conversely, revealed Beckett's profound indebtness to Shakespeare.

When Kott started to write his essays, the wave of the drama of the absurd was reaching its climax, and sophisticated audiences in Paris, London, or New York were applauding the plays of the Romanian-born Eugène Ionesco or the Irish-born Beckett. To fit Shakespeare for this new fashion required a good deal of imagination and adaptation and sometimes some clever juggling but it suited the needs of many theatres intent on presenting an up-to-date repertoire of both contemporary and classical plays. Consequently, Kott's book had a great impact on many Shakespearian productions in the 1960s and 1970s, including some of the most notable: Peter Brook's *King Lear* (both on the stage, 1962–4, and on the screen, 1969), his *Midsummer Night's Dream* (staged 1970), or Peter Hall and John Barton's adaptation of the early histories called *The Wars of the Roses* (1963, televised 1965).

In Eastern Europe, Kott's essays played an additional role by offering an alternative to propagandist appropriations of Shakespeare. Freely using the tenets of existentialist philosophy or Freudian psychoanalysis and the devices of the drama of the absurd, they cast doubt upon the favourite Communist notion that Shakespeare's dramas affirmed a positive view of humanity which transcended class bounds and anticipated a socialist culture. Kott's one-sided readings of Shakespeare's comedies as bitter, cruel, and brutally erotic contradicted the equally one-sided proclamations of those Marxists who asserted that Shakespeare's positive heroes with their optimism and enthusiasm, their vitality and courage, made a direct appeal to a youthful and vigorous society which was transforming the lives of its people on the basis of a rational system of planning.

In February 1964, Jan Kott gave a talk in Prague and had a reunion with Peter Brook and the Royal Shakespeare Company who played their *King Lear* and *The Comedy of Errors* at the Czech National Theatre. The first breezes of the Prague Spring of 1968 were in the air, and liberal Marxists were developing their concept of socialism with a human face, introducing tolerance and plurality into all spheres of life. Whereas in frozen Moscow Kott's essays were banned by Communist authorities and circulated only in *samizdat* (home-made, clandestine copies), they were published in Czech translation and started to be used by many Czech and Slovak directors as a sort of new theatrical gospel. During the Shakespeare quatercentenary organized by Charles University in April 1964, Kott's book was freely discussed by several speakers. His mistakes in literary facts, poor knowledge of Shakespearian scholarship, and misreadings of Shakespeare's text were subjected to detailed criticism but his general approach was appreciated in one of the keynote lectures as a liberating incentive to overcome all forms of stagnation and dogmatism.

Kott's essays were translated into many languages, among them Slovak, Slovene, Serbo-Croatian, Hungarian, and Romanian. In the long run, they turned paradoxically into a new kind of dogma, being used by less creative directors as a violently anti-Romantic imperative of contemporariness. The situation was acutely described in a review essay on *The Tempest* which was performed by a travelling company moving in a ship along the coast of Croatia in 1980 and 1981:

Watching the production . . . I had the impression that the artistic director of the company simply allowed the play to unravel itself naturally. This is a salutary tendency in view of the fact that most Zagreb directors usually start with an idea, almost always borrowed from Jan Kott, impose it upon the play, and then proclaim it a contemporary, and the only correct, version of Shakespeare.[6]

About that time, Kott himself visited the Croatian (or Illyrian) coast and saw *Hamlet* performed in modern dress at the castle of the predominantly Renaissance Dubrovnik. He was struck by the discrepancy between Claudius' court dressed in modern costumes and the Ghost, who looked 'quite ridiculous' in the contemporary setting. Recalling the Dubrovnik production at a conference in London by the end of the 1980s, Kott admitted that 'Shakespeare could have been our contemporary twenty-five years ago, whereas he is not so much of a contemporary today', adding with an endearing and disarming self-irony: 'In some ways, I feel like a ghost myself.'[7]

III

Another approach to Shakespeare as our contemporary was practised in the Soviet Union by the film and theatre director Grigori Kozintsev (born in 1905 in the Ukrainian capital Kiev, died 1973). His productions of *King Lear* and *Othello* during the Second World War and his *Hamlet* in Pasternak's translation right after Stalin's death have already been discussed. In 1962 Kozintsev published his first full-length book on Shakespeare under the title *Our Contemporary: William Shakespeare*, which was the Russian equivalent to the French title of Kott's essays published in Paris in the same year.[8] The coincidence was not accidental: both authors wanted to stress their closeness to Shakespeare by calling him a man of our time. Kozintsev, however, felt the closeness not in Shakespeare's similarity to the theatre of the absurd but in his capacity to stir our conscience, to defend man against all forms of inhumanity, to discover 'the unmasked face of Virtue and of Scorn' in individuals and the whole society. Ostensibly condemning the Nazi terror, he was equally concerned about the immediate Stalinist past. He was a Marxist, convinced of the justice and humanity of socialism, but, for that very reason, he became an anti-Stalinist.

In his films, productions, essays, and books, Kozintsev developed the best features of Russian culture from the eighteenth century to his own time. His sensitivity to Shakespeare's poetry and to the infinite variety of Shakespeare's characters prevented him from any simplified or violent modernization, even though he started his career, as a very young man in 1922, by running a workshop called the Factory of the Eccentric Actor, in which he suggested trying out a modern tempo and performing *Hamlet* in a compressed pantomime. When he was commissioned to film *Hamlet* in 1962 (to be released in 1964), he was already famous for his co-direction of a film trilogy called *Maxim* (1935, 1937, 1939), depicting the struggles of a Russian worker from the beginning of the twentieth century to the 1917 October Revolution, and for his film *Don Quixote* (1957).

In his diary notes about his 'Work on the Movie', concluding his first book, he paid tribute to Laurence Olivier's *Hamlet* film but pointed out that 'Olivier cut the theme of government which I find extremely interesting'. Following the Russian tradition, he paid close attention to the 'Time, the historical process, society' in which the tragic hero had to live. There were three layers of time fused in his film: the ancient time of the mysterious and majestic Ghost; the Renaissance time of young Hamlet's humanistic Wittenberg and Claudius' anti-humanistic, power-usurping Elsinore; and our present time, fraught with the traumatic experiences of both Hitler's Holocaust and Stalin's Gulag, alleviated by Khrushchev's precarious thaw. Contemporary associations were strengthened by the casting of Innokenti Smoktunovski in the role of the Prince: this handsome and charismatic actor had survived imprisonment both by the Germans in the Second World War and then by the Stalinist penal cohorts. To him it was not Denmark which was a prison.

Searching for a 'poetic expression of time', Kozintsev decided that the tragedy should be given characteristic features of the Renaissance in costumes and interiors, while nature should be elemental: sea crashing against rocks and the ramparts of a daunting castle, bleak northern sea-coast, sky covered with threatening clouds but breathtaking at dawn, recurrent fire in torches and hearths, a solitary seagull reappearing in long flights, symbolizing freedom and high aspirations of the human spirit as well as the arts (a seagull has been the emblem of the MAT company for decades).

Against this background, characters and their fates were not only contemporary but decidedly Russian. The whole film grew into a poetic tragedy of humanism and individual conscience, reflecting the feelings and thoughts of a Russian intellectual confronted with a totalitarian state. At the same time, Kozintsev insisted on 'the inexhaustibility' of Shakespeare's text: 'People of various eras and talents have tried to establish one single theme for explaining *Hamlet*. But Shakespeare wrote life, which contained an infinite swarm of seeds for ever new ideas.'

Kozintsev found the strongest inspiration for his 'cinematographic poetry' in Galina Ulanova: 'Her Juliet is the finest ever done, a truly Shakespearian heroine, although she utters not a word. Her art *is* poetry and therefore you don't try to remember the verses. Her triumph is due to her having danced the role through. A new fabric was formed of her own harmony.'

A perfect example of Kozintsev's creative transformation of Shakespeare's poetry and Ulanova's ballet art into his own filmic poem was his introduction of Ophelia in a short scene which he called 'The Dance Lesson'. Although Ophelia's outward image was suggested by Botticelli, El Greco (hands), and Picasso's blue period, the warping of her character was represented by a lesson in which an old governess taught her how to dance, how to smile, how to turn into an obedient doll in the hands of her father and the whole corrupt court.

The great care given to this sequence can be seen from Kozintsev's exchange of letters with Dmitri Shostakovich. Kozintsev asked the composer to write a short piece to be used by the instructress during her lesson to Ophelia. When Shostakovich heard the soundtrack of his music, he decided to change the violin and the accompanying piano to a lute, played by the old woman, accompanied by a celesta. Suddenly, the tinkling metallic sounds of the antique instrument struck the right note. Kozintsev commented on the whole creative process: 'The work of the composer was similar to getting the focus in photography. He had now found a completely accurate sound image.' In the rest of his score, Shostakovich was encouraged by Kozintsev to feel free to shape his musical text 'outside the framework of the Shakespearian epoch', so that he could develop his own vigorous style to reinforce or counterpoint the rhythmic movements of the action in over half the shots.

Ophelia's dancing lesson marked the beginning of the deformation of her essentially sweet nature into 'a mechanical plaything' that could be further forced 'to renounce love and to look for a dirty trick in everything'. Step by step, she was driven into madness in which, paradoxically, she found happiness. Her fate suggested that for weaker characters mad society offered madness and suicide as the only ways of escape. During her derangement, the tinkling tones of the Dance Lesson interrupted her own singing.

Darker aspects in the character of Prince Hamlet were reduced by both Smoktunovski's noble, elegant acting and Boris Pasternak's screenplay in which his translation was substantially abridged. The main line of the hero's action, however, was preserved to portray him as an unyielding judge of his time and pioneer of the future. In his dramatic entrance, he was shown galloping over a massive drawbridge which was immediately raised to trap him in the jaws of Elsinore. Claudius' court appeared stately and luxurious, but it was full of puppets and spies. Hamlet delivered his first soliloquy in voice-over as an interior monologue, while he strode through a crush of obsequious courtiers against the background of music and the noise of a court reception. His later soliloquies also were presented as interior monologues, following his own words 'But break, my heart, for I must hold my tongue' (1.2.159). His isolation was not physical but spiritual: he stood alone in the crowd of Pharisees. Only Horatio's friendship and the visit and vigorous performance of the strolling players were a great support in his struggle against the tyrant and his stooges.

Departing from his 1954 stage production, Kozintsev decided to follow Pasternak's vision of the ending of the tragedy as life's general continuation after the silence of isolated death. Hamlet's corpse was carried by Fortinbras's captains to the tones of a funeral march until it disappeared in a crowd of common people gathered outside the walls of Elsinore to mourn silently the death of their beloved Prince. The last verbal message of the tragedy was Hamlet's parting words 'The rest is silence'. Their foregrounded deliverance has been interpreted by different film critics in different ways: as a fatalistic confirmation of political hopelessness or a stoic response to the tragic time. No doubt, they made the ending of the tragedy questioningly ambiguous. They brought to mind Sumarokov's eighteenth-century *Hamlet* in which the theme of conscience, the concern for the response of the people, and the ambiguity of the ending were prominent. Although Kozintsev did not name Sumarokov among his predecessors, the Russian roots of his film may be traced as far back as that. More directly, the inspiration can be derived from Pushkin's *Boris Godunov*, which ends with the people receiving the news of the death of Tsar Boris's son and wife in astonished silence.

Hamlet's last words and the fade-out of the funeral procession were followed by another flight of a seagull over the sea and a blazing torch of fire, seeming to suggest life-giving, Promethean heat. The images of fire were, along with the flights of the seagull, the most frequent shots of the whole film. They represented Kozintsev's cinematographic response to Shakespeare's favourite poetic device—his iterative imagery.

While Kozintsev's *Hamlet* closed with the hero's dead body disappearing slowly in a crowd of silent people, his *King Lear* (1970) opened with another long line of poor peasants toiling up a rocky hillside leading towards Lear's castle. They were summoned to hear the king's decree about the division of his state. As the almighty Lear, enraged by Cordelia's plain words, screamed his fury against his daughter, he strutted and fretted on the battlements while the people below threw themselves prostrate to the ground, frightened by the dragon's wrath. The contrast between the long shot of the wild, puny figure and the inflated image of a godlike ruler, reflected both in his own and the people's illusion, was alarming.[9] Only in the storm, when he tore off his mask of power together with his clothes, did Lear's real face become visible: suffering had made him 'beautiful and human'.[10]

Kozintsev took great pains to find the right face for his Lear. He liked to say that the chief advantage of the cinema over the theatre was not that you could have galloping horses but that you could look closer into a man's eyes. After many auditions, he chose an Estonian actor, Yuri Yarvet, whose delicate Baltic features were able to express all the stirrings of Lear's passions. Like Mikhoels at the Moscow Jewish Theatre in 1936, Yarvet and Kozintsev decided that Lear would not wear a conventional long patriarchal beard which would tend to camouflage his feelings.

Looking for an appropriate landscape and atmosphere for his vision of the tragedy, Kozintsev resolved not to delocalize the space and clear the screen of the traces of history, as Peter Brook did in his *Lear* film (although otherwise he held Brook's stage and film productions in high esteem). He was convinced that he could not fully follow the fate of the king without simultaneously showing the plight of his subjects. The wide-screen format seemed to invite him to such a broad canvas:

'Lear in the thick of life—this is what the cinema could add to what we knew already, to what the theatre had already revealed.' In this endeavour, Kozintsev was anxious to avoid any signs of the pompous settings of conventional historical or pseudohistorical films. Only 'real materials', such as wood, iron, leather, or fur, would do. For similar reasons, he relied on the experience of his *Hamlet* film and shot in black and white, not in colour, adding in his modest way: 'I do not know what colour grief is, or what shades suffering has. I wanted to trust Shakespeare and the audience: it is shameful to sugar *Lear* with beautiful effects.'

Lear's stormy progress from wrath and pride to humility, discovery of truth about himself and his subjects, and final devotion to his truthful daughter formed the core of Kozintsev's film. One of the most powerful sequences took place in the storm-pelted hovel on the heath, which was occupied not only by the mad Poor Tom, as in Shakespeare, but also by a small commune of homeless cripples and beggars to whom Lear addressed his prayer face to face. After the defeat of Cordelia's army, she and Lear were led away as prisoners but they looked quietly happy and victorious: they had won their inner freedom amidst the cruelty and devastation of the world.

In his talk given in 1971 at the first World Shakespeare Congress in Vancouver, where his *Lear* film was first released and rewarded by a long, standing ovation, Kozintsev argued: 'In the contemporary theatre the element of cruelty in this tragedy is often intensified. It is most certainly there, and on a vast scale. But *King Lear* is not only "Theatre of Cruelty" but also "Theatre of Mercy". The play's foreground is occupied by the figures of Cordelia, Edgar, and the Fool.'[11]

The Fool's role was foregrounded from the very beginning to the very end of the film. Kozintsev admitted that he could not bear losing the Fool halfway through the play because he grew very fond of him, especially in the interpretation of the actor Oleg Dal. Even before the first entrance of the almighty King, the Fool's bells jingled gently as 'a tongue stuck out at pomposity and grandiloquence'. They resounded softly but persistently even during the storm, as the call of conscience. In agreement with composer Dmitri Shostakovich, the other particular sound of the film was not lofty fanfares or the roll of drums but the soft note of a wooden pipe, which the Fool has made for himself to cure his master's madness. During the battle scenes, a requiem sung by a chorus broke out in contrast to the butchery and destruction of war, then it fell silent. Once again, the Fool's pipe prevailed, providing the tonal farewell of the tragedy. Kozintsev confessed: 'The cry of grief, bursting through the dumbness of the ages, through the deafness of time, must be heard. We made the film with the very purpose that it should be heard.'

Kozintsev and Dal presented the Fool as a downtrodden, ragged boy with a shaven head and childlike, tormented eyes; but he was clever, talented, and able to glimpse the truth of life in any situation. He articulated, in his own grotesque way, the feelings of the 'poor naked wretches' of Lear's kingdom. Sticking it out with his master to the end, kicked aside by soldiers who carried the corpses of Lear and his three daughters, he mourned his master's death amidst the crowd of country people as a village Fool of Christ. One was reminded of Pushkin's *Boris Godunov* with the Idiot Nikolka, who was probably inspired by Lear's Fool. It is possible to follow Shakespeare's Fool migrating to Pushkin and then, in Russian garb, on to Kozintsev's film.

A complete identification with the poor naked wretches was achieved by Edgar, as he transformed himself into Poor Tom and joined a long struggling line of the dispossessed of Lear's kingdom. The sequence of mad Tom leading his cruelly blinded father Gloucester cannot be easily forgotten. Not finding an adequate cinematic representation of Gloucester's attempted suicidal leap from the imaginary cliff of Dover, Kozintsev cut it, compensating for it by a close-up of the dying blind Gloucester recognizing his son Edgar by touch. In this serene scene of recognition and reconciliation, which is only narrated in the play (5.3.173–90), Kozintsev fulfilled, in filmic terms, Gloucester's pious wish to see his true son in his touch (4.1.23).

Edgar's duel with his treacherous stepbrother Edmund was presented as a victory of truth over reckless careerism and acquisitiveness. Edmund had behind him all the newly acquired might of his social position and his army but he finally collapsed when confronted with the arm of justice. It was significant that the final sequence of the film was concentrated on Edgar's quiet, purposeful face and figure. Although Albany shaped up in the film as an upright and energetic man, Kozintsev decided not to give him the final quatrain, as it was translated by Pasternak according to the Quarto edition, but to prefer the Folio reading and show Edgar accepting, without words, the 'weight of this sad time' and leaving to join other people around him to extinguish the fires and clear the debris of war. Such an ending suggested that Lear's and Gloucester's legacy would not be forgotten, because it was Edgar who shared, in the guise of Poor Tom, the experience of the houseless wretches and who was close to both Lear and Gloucester at their penetrating moments of social insight.

The most lasting memories of the film, however, return to Lear and Cordelia, although the sight of her dead body hanging high in the air was shocking and only the reappearance of her sweet face in Lear's embrace alleviated the pain. As to Lear, the final evaluation can best be left to Kozintsev himself: 'This man remains in our memory lit by bursts of lightning, a grey-haired rebel who accuses injustice and demands that the world change or cease.'

Kozintsev expressed this vision of Lear in his first book on Shakespeare. His second, which proved to be even more profound and moving, appeared only after his premature death, under the title *King Lear: The Space of Tragedy* (in Russian 1973, in English 1977). I have used some of its ideas in discussing the film, but the whole text is infinitely richer. I can only agree with an American scholar who called it an 'astonishing book . . . unmatched as a record of a film director's artistic struggles . . . one of the great works of this century'.[12]

Kozintsev died suddenly in harness. Most of the numerous notes and sketches preserved in his study are concerned with his plans for filming Gogol's tales, Pushkin's little tragedies, the story of Lev Tolstoy's last pilgrimage, and three plays by Shakespeare: *As You Like It* ('a play about emigration'), *Measure for Measure*, and *The Tempest*. The quite detailed notes on the latter play bear witness to his fascination with the theme of parting with the arts and life altogether. The most striking idea is the inclusion of Prospero among Shakespeare's tragic heroes as an exile, magus, and poet whose humanistic ideals are brutally shattered by the European civilization of scheming, murdering politicians and drunken plebeians. Kozintsev believed that Prospero bore strong autobiographical features of the ageing Shakespeare, tired of words, words, words, of selling his art to both noble patrons and noisy groundlings. Behind the image of the despairing Prospero–Shakespeare, one can divine the conscience of Kozintsev himself, deeply disturbed by developments in the Soviet Union and the whole Soviet bloc after the invasion of Czechoslovakia in 1968. Kozintsev's anxiety and distress went so far that he probably considered supplementing his screenplay of *The Tempest* with Macbeth's most pessimistic soliloquy (5.5.18–27). Several Russian variants of it have been found among his *Tempest* papers.[13] For an artist of such a sensitive conscience, the stagnating dictatorship and rampant militarism of the Brezhnev period must have appeared indeed as a tale

> Told by an idiot, full of sound and fury,
> Signifying nothing.

IV

To realize the stifling effects of Brezhnev's leadership, we must return to the flowering and sudden crushing of the Prague Spring of 1968 (later recognized by Mikhail Gorbachev as the precursor of his perestroika). The whole liberating movement in Czechoslovakia started in the early 1960s; it was anticipated and supported by radically new cultural trends, including productions of Shakespeare. Perhaps the most innovative was *Romeo and Juliet* at the National Theatre in Prague, introduced into the repertory in the season 1963–4 as a contribution to the Czech quatercentenary celebrations of Shakespeare's birth. There was, however, not a trace of the Romantic or neo-Romantic jubilees of yore in this production. The old stylized speeches, faces, costumes, and sets were of no use in the roaring sea of troubles and violent clashes between the old and young generations. The anger, the nervous agitation, the agonized rashness of the youth of the 1960s, but also their pure passion and readiness for self-sacrifice, were constantly breaking into the classic story. In conspicuous departure from the productions of the 1950s, in which Romeo's denunciation of money during his encounter with the Apothecary in Mantua (5.1.60–84) was given special prominence, a new key topos, opening the play, was found in Romeo's threatening words at Juliet's tomb:

> The time and my intents are savage-wild,
> More fierce and more inexorable far
> Than empty tigers or the roaring sea. (5.3.37–9)

The whole production voiced an impatient and impassioned protest against the futile grudge and cold-hearted cruelty of the old generation who had turned the world into a battlefield, where 'civil blood makes civil hands unclean'. Above the hatred and slanging matches of the old world, free love, free speech, but also human tolerance and mutual understanding were stressed as the highest values.

The director of the production, Otomar Krejča, could rely on an equally innovative stage designer, Josef Svoboda, who used the advances of modern technology to achieve the quick changes of locale of the Elizabethan theatre. His central stage unit was an invisibly supported white arcaded gallery that appeared floating in the air, representing alternatively Renaissance windows in the background or, slid into a forward position, Juliet's balcony, the symbol of love. The lighting, marking the different hours of day and night, gave the performance a dreamlike quality, similar to Svoboda's effects in his experimental multi-media Prague theatre Laterna Magika.

After the Soviet-led invasion of Czechoslovakia in 1968, Krejča's work was gradually suppressed, but he won further success in Western Europe. Svoboda achieved international acclaim all over Europe as well as in North and South America, while he also managed to continue working at home. His two stage designs for *Hamlet* at the Prague National Theatre (1959–66, 1982–8) have become legendary. In the first, step units were surrounded by twenty tall vertical panels covered with black plastic material. They shifted rapidly with each change of scene into different patterns, dimly reflecting halberds, swords, cups, or bodies in motion. This labyrinthine shaping of space created the atmosphere of an alienated world in mysterious light. The Ghost appeared only as a whirl of spotlights abruptly transfixed high up on the black background as a pair of eyes. During his central soliloquy, Hamlet was shown in silhouette, illuminated from behind by light reflected from one of the panels. The production was full of questions and unresolved problems. Only Hamlet himself found his way through the shifting and slippery world to fulfil his duty as 'heaven's scourge and minister', killing Claudius in an elated peace of mind.

The second *Hamlet* production also employed stepped platforms, surrounded this time by nothing but heavy, black velvet drapes. Most of the action occurred on an extended forestage, where Hamlet could feel in close contact with his audience. The revelation of the full space of the tragedy was deferred until the ending: Claudius, groping desperately for help before Hamlet's ferocious attack, tore down the black drapery and died among the tatters, pinned down for what he was:

Fig. 3. *Hamlet* (Prague National Theatre, 1959), designed by Josef Svoboda

'a king of shreds and patches'. The horizon, so dramatically lifted, revealed a steep black staircase on which the body of the Prince was slowly carried by four captains to the top of the steps, as if elevated to the heavens, high above the corpses of Claudius, Gertrude, and Laertes. This was Svoboda's homage to both Hamlet and Gordon Craig's vision of the tragic hero as the great cleanser of the world whose free spirit could not be bound and covered by earth.[14]

The whole period of the Prague Spring lasted much longer than its metaphoric name suggested. It was preceded by a massive anti-Soviet revolt in Hungary in 1956 and a decade of gestation; after its suppression by an enormous military force in August 1968, it went into hiding but survived spiritually and culturally in a variety of forms. Although the streets and squares of Prague were watched by tanks, the walls and fences kept on being covered by protesting graffiti, some of them displaying typically Czech gallows humour: 'Red brothers, go home to your reservations!' or 'Lenin awake, Brezhnev has gone mad!' In January 1969, a student of Charles University, Jan Palach, burnt himself to death in a desperate attempt to bolster up the flagging resistance.

At exactly the same time, *Timon of Athens* had its première at the theatre on the Balustrade in the historic heart of Prague. The theatre was founded at the end of 1958 as a small experimental studio of both drama and pantomime but it soon emerged as a daringly avant-garde playhouse, best known for introducing to Czechoslovakia the drama of the absurd of both foreign and domestic provenance (Alfred Jarry, Eugène Ionesco, Samuel Beckett, Václav Havel). Since all absurd plays were forbidden after the Soviet occupation, their role was taken over by *Timon*, presented as Shakespeare's 'most satirical and, in his own way, most absurd play…the tragedy of lost illusions and abysmal disillusion'. Without toning down Marx's favourite passages on the corrupting, poisonous power of gold (4.3.25–45, 384–94), the chief corruption was revealed in the betrayal of friendship which, after all, is the essential concern of the play:

> Breath infect breath,
> That their society, as their friendship, may
> Be merely poison! (4.1.30–2)

After decades of Communist propaganda extolling Soviet–Czecho-slovak friendship in innumerable official speeches and pamphlets, these words blew on the audiences like a spine-chilling Siberian gust. To point up the protest against the tanks imposing order on the occupied country, a rhymed couplet was added at the end of Act 3, Scene 1:

> Those that have power to hurt and smother
> Will heap one injury upon another.[15]

Timon emerged in the second part of the play as a half naked, chained saint in the woods, an unrelenting critic of corrupted and perverse human relations. But he died in a grotesquely erotic dance of death with a voluptuous whore who finally revealed a skull beneath her mask. A closing pantomime was added in which the bit part of the Fool was extended: he reappeared, holding Timon's chains in his arms.

Similar approaches to Shakespeare were developed in other productions at the Balustrade theatre: *The Tempest* (1975), *Hamlet* (1978), and *Macbeth* (1981). The most significant was *Hamlet* under the direction of Evald Schorm, who used the heavily abridged and garbled text of the First Quarto to produce a swiftly moving play with striking effects. The first surprise came with the Ghost, whose creaking armour and heavy bandages soaked in blood pointed to a travesty of the Elizabethan 'bloody tragedy'. This impression was strengthened by the rudimentary setting of white vertical panels spattered with blood. Gradually it dawned upon the audience that the whole play was meant to oscillate between farce and tragedy, approaching the modern genre of tragic grotesque, which had become one of the hallmarks of the Balustrade Company's artistic vision and expression.

Young Hamlet, in black jeans and sweater, behaved in quite a calm manner, but spoke daggers most of the time. His final act of revenge received a surprising support: during his duel with Laertes, the gravediggers reappeared to take hold of King Claudius, tossing him back and forth and eventually presenting him to victorious Hamlet as the final target. Even more surprisingly, the gravediggers continued to dominate the whole ending of the play. They were not presented as sturdy, staunch representatives of the people but as modern circus clowns in white face with glaring red plastic balls for noses; they wore the black rubber boots and gloves, long rubberized aprons, and paramilitary peaked caps of a sanitation unit. One of them dragged the corpses of Ophelia and Polonius back on stage, adding them to the dead bodies of the King, the Queen, Laertes, and Hamlet himself. The other gravedigger, softly whistling and humming to himself with malicious relish, pulled down a military camouflage net, which had been suspended above the stage from the beginning, and carefully spread it over all the dead bodies, dusting them with disinfectant powder.

Here the tragedy of the great and mighty was seen, with devastating effect, from below, as from a frog's eye view. The final arrival of Fortinbras, for whom the gravediggers did not give a fig, could not alleviate the shock received from the image of a mass grave, reminiscent of massacres of our time.

This was a raw, underdone *Hamlet*, with blood dripping from wide-gaping wounds in both bodies and souls, and the clowns lapping it up with infantile delight. The revolt of the student Prince ended up absurdly in the lower depths of society. There was no upward turn, no hope because Fortinbras did not promise to be anything more than a puppet ruler.

Shattered as the performance left us, we yet felt a peculiar relief, a kind of modern absurd catharsis. Only years later was this complex and perplexed feeling illuminated by the insight of our master-absurdist Václav Havel, who started as a stage-hand at the Balustrade to become its most promising playwright, then a dissident, and finally our President: 'Who knows whether hopelessness is not the innermost source of real human hope and whether without experiencing the absurdity of the world one can anticipate, look for, and find its sense.'[16]

Another confrontational, dissenting *Hamlet* was produced in Moscow's off-centre studio theatre called Taganka, since it was founded in 1946 at Taganka Square. Its flowering started in 1964, when it was taken over by a group of avant-garde actors led by Yuri Lyubimov. In 1971, they introduced their *Hamlet* with the protest singer and poet Vladimir Vysotsky in the title part. The production became famous as 'Hamlet with a guitar' and remained in repertory until Vysotsky's early death in 1980.

It opened on a bare stage with Hamlet in turtleneck and slacks in the background, playing his guitar and astounding the gathering audience by suddenly running up to front-stage and starting to chant the opening lines of his key, reiterated soliloquy 'To be or not to be' in the style of a rock singer. According to other reports, his opening text was Pasternak's poem 'Hamlet' from the epilogue to the novel *Doctor Zhivago*, which was at that time still banned in the Soviet Union. Apparently, Vysotsky alternated the two openings during the many runs of the production.

The gravediggers were also shifted from their late appearance in the play to the very beginning to add a visual foreground to Vysotsky's singing. They were unmistakably Russian peasants, swigging vodka, shovelling real earth, and extracting real skulls as they dug the grave for Hamlet's father. The grave remained there throughout the play, and the gravediggers with the skulls reappeared from time to time to make the spectators think of death (and possibly move them to be more decent in their lives, as Lyubimov remarked).

The chief scenic device was a huge curtain knitted of coarse wool and hemp, hanging from a pivot and track system which allowed it to move in all directions. It was both more dynamic and more potent than the rather static iron curtain of Okhlopkov's 1954 *Hamlet*. It could sweep actors completely aside as non-persons or support them in their positions, for instance when it was turned into Claudius' throne. Its dominating, sinister, and implacable function became most visible and palpable in the ending, when it swept up all the corpses and survivors left on stage, indifferent to human life or death, and finally advanced towards the audience, threatening to destroy them, too.

Vysotsky's Hamlet was simple, mournful, and full of thoughts of death. Only occasionally did he burst into frantic action, being gripped by a searing thirst to avenge not only his father but all the victims of Claudius' usurpation and oppression. The long shadows of Stalin's criminal dictatorship and Brezhnev's aggression were falling on the stage. Although the production was tolerated for a surprisingly long time, possibly as a kind of safety valve for theatrical dissent, and in 1976 was even allowed to participate in the World Theatre Festival in Belgrade to demonstrate Brezhnev's inclination toward cultural and political détente, it undoubtedly became one of the causes of Lyubimov's exile in 1984. When Lyubimov revived it in 1989, in Vysotsky's memory, for a tour in Britain with a British cast, it proved to be remarkable again but also proved how difficult it was to transplant Russian idiosyncrasies into foreign soil.

From among the hundreds of theatres spread all over the vast territories of the former Soviet Union, at least one more deserves to be marked out for its Shakespearian productions. In Tbilisi, the capital of Georgia, a National Theatre was founded in the 1880s and reorganized in the Soviet era under the name of the eighteenth-century national poet Rustaveli. In spite of the inhuman persecution of some Georgian Shakespearian translators, actors, and directors by the two most infamous Georgians in history, Stalin and Beria, the Rustaveli Theatre managed to keep up its high artistic standard and, after Stalin's and Beria's deaths, regained full vigour. Its best Shakespearian director, Robert Sturua, won almost unanimous acclaim when he was allowed to première his production of *Richard III* at the Edinburgh International Festival in 1979, to return to Britain for a second tour, and to take part in the highly successful 1981 audio-visual season of the Avignon Festival.

Bringing out the cynical, ironical, and comic features in Richard's character and the whole play, Sturua presented a fascinating, crudely dynamic mixture of tragedy and farce, drama and melodrama, cruelty and tomfoolery, savage rat race for power and Saturnalian relief. The white space of the stage swarmed with grotesque, bloodstained or deathly white-faced figures, recalling Hieronymus Bosch's paintings or Goya's etchings *Los Caprichos*. The incidental music offered a similarly provocative blend of rock and roll, sentimental pop-song, political anthem, Bach, Mozart, and Gounod.

The title part was taken by Ramaz Chkhikvadze, who rejected the traditional conception of Richard as a romantic heroic villain and went so far as to deny the time-honoured image of him with a humped back. Instead, he wore a grey Napoleonic overcoat covering a heavy, strangely lame body. His face was most horrifying when he was friendly or amorous, giving the smile of a shark. With his motionless, bloodshot eyes and thin blue lips, he kissed Lady Anne in the wooing scene as if sucking blood from her neck. In fact, he was far less attracted by the lady than by the crown, which hypnotized him: he stared at it for a long time silently, in a sort of torpor, before finally grabbing it, putting it on his head and pulling it over his eyes with both hands. He was both a Fascist or Stalinist Napoleon and a clown.

From the opening of the play, Richard was closely followed by a beautiful, almost angelic youth dressed in a long white coat. This was Richmond, who finally killed Richard to become the first Tudor King Henry VII. Yet even this glorious uniter of the White and the Red Rose fell victim, in Sturua's finale, to the universal lust for power. Staring at the crown exactly as Richard had done earlier, the young king ascended the throne to the same coaxingly sentimental tune which had heralded Richard's entrance on stage. At the same time, a rosy-cheeked clown, who had been introduced into the play in the last phases of Richard's rule as the King's grotesque alter ego, moved across the stage up to the platform. Dancing lightly, he approached the audience with a mocking wink indicating that the snow-white hero Henry will not prove any better than the 'bloody dog' Richard.[17]

All this was shown not as something bizarre and remote but as a horridly living present, a scenic metaphor of twentieth-century savagery, of the acquisitive drives in any individual, any nation, and any state, East or West. Sturua offered a key to his interpretation in his talk at the World Shakespeare Congress at Stratford-upon-Avon in 1981: 'Mixing heterogeneous elements and tendencies, comedy and tragedy, past and present, brings enrichment but also conflict. It is very difficult to master all this in one play but when it succeeds it turns out to be extremely effective—at least for me.'

Besides this modest statement of method Sturua also revealed his chief theoretical inspiration: 'The greatest impact on me as director was made by Mikhail Bakhtin and his book on Rabelais. I could not possibly accommodate my production of *Richard III* to all the incentives coming from Bakhtin's theory but at least I tried to evoke the carnival atmosphere.' Effectively using some essential ideas of Bakhtin's theory of the popular roots of Renaissance culture, Sturua offered a spectacular show, combining political message and pointedly theatrical entertainment in the best Brechtian style.

V

The art and the mind of the German dramatist, theatre director, theoretician, and poet Bertolt (or Bert) Brecht (1898–1956) made themselves fully felt in theatres all over Europe and America after the Second World War, when he returned from his exile in the United States to East Germany, but he started to develop them soon after the First World War, especially after he became assistant to Max Reinhardt in Berlin. To trace his artistic growth, we must return as far back as that, because some of his most original ideas sprang from his early experience with the English drama, while he was reading, adapting, and directing Marlowe, Shakespeare, and Gay.

In his radical departure from the classical five-act structure and the modern well-made play, he was inspired by the unfettered and often contrastive sequence of scenes of the English chronicle play to create his 'epic drama', marked by a dialectically narrated action in which each scene contributed to a kind of free montage. Similarly, his other famous theatrical devices, his 'alienation' or 'estrangement' effects, were partly based on the Elizabethan non-illusionist stage; Brecht found Shakespeare 'full of alienation effects' which contradicted the neo-Aristotelian notion that drama should imitate reality by creating an illusion of it. He preferred Shakespeare's unlocalized, empty stage with just a few but significant props, white, even light, and stylized acting. Instead of penetrating into the souls of the heroes and heroines by Stanislavsky's method, Brecht concentrated on telling stories and promoting in both his actors and spectators critical attitudes to plots and characters. Like Shakespeare, he used prologues, epilogues, asides, and direct addresses to the audience, allusions to current events, and songs deliberately interrupting the flow of action.

He did not see Shakespeare as our contemporary; on the contrary, he insisted on playing him historically in full contrast to our own time, leaving the audience to discover both the dissimilarities and the closeness between Shakespeare and themselves. He taught that spectators should be left to use their own reason and judgement, to which he appealed more than to their feelings. While expecting audiences to derive their enjoyment from their active participation in the performance, he did not hesitate to prod them in what he believed to be the right direction: the Marxist interpretation of the liberation struggle of the exploited classes as the basic force of historical progress. In this way, a tension arose between Brecht's avant-garde aesthetic and his rather rigid ideology. That is why he is sometimes called a great Marxist artist or alternatively a great artist despite his didactic Marxism.

While drawing on the Shakespearian model to form his theatre theory, Brecht reworked Shakespeare's plays into various German versions. His early adaptations of *Macbeth* and *Hamlet* for German radio (1927, 1931) have not been preserved, because he had to leave Germany in haste when Hitler came to dictatorial power in 1933. Before that, Brecht started to modernize and adapt *Measure for Measure*, and his several workings resulted in a complete transformation called ironically *The Roundheads and the Peakheads*. It ridiculed Hitler's racial division of people into Aryans and Jews and was first produced in Danish during Brecht's exile in Copenhagen in 1936. Although the first night was a success, the theatre was soon picketed by Fascist agitators bearing anti-Semitic posters, and the production was taken off when most critics found it too tendentious.

Preserving the skeletons of Shakespeare's plots about a deputy ruler appointed to enforce strict government and about a virgin implored by her brother to save his life by sacrificing her chastity, the play presents Angelo Iberin (Shakespeare's puritanical deputy Angelo) as a droll but not deadly dangerous demagogue whose sexual desire is diverted from women to a lust for power, signified in one scene by a microphone. His role is diminished, and the central conflict develops between the poor peasantry and landlords who use Angelo Iberin as an instrument for splitting class solidarity by racial prejudice.

The main purpose of the play was to demonstrate that the rich stick together in preserving their government, suppressing rebellions of the poor, and preparing wars against foreign enemies, the Squareheads. Although Brecht called it a 'horror tale', its anti-Hitler satire proved rather naïve when it was later confronted with the real horrors of Nazism. That is probably the main reason why it has been revived only rarely.

Brecht had to change his place of exile more often than his shoes, as he put it in one of his poems. Moving to Sweden, he wrote several prose scenes to be inserted into *Macbeth*, *Hamlet*, and *Romeo and Juliet* and used, along with other exercises, by his wife, the actress Helene Weigel, who taught dramatic art in Stockholm. The aim of the short interludes was to train rehearsing actors in alienation, in taking critical attitudes to their characters, and thus playing them better, in their full, complex, and contradictory natures. For *Romeo and Juliet* two interludes were needed to show, with sparkling irony, how each of the lovers was consumed by passion and idealistic notions of great love to the extent of ignoring the needs of their servants or retainers. For this purpose, Brecht added two characters: a poor tenant-farmer who is heartlessly treated by Romeo and an unhappy maid whose own meeting with her lover is selfishly thwarted by Juliet. It was provocative to introduce sharp social conflicts and a biting bit of common sense into Shakespeare's most famous love story, but the device seems far-fetched. Such conflicts could have been derived directly from Shakespeare's text: from Juliet's rows with the Nurse or Romeo's encounter with the starving Apothecary in Mantua. Fortunately, in his own plays, such as *The Life of Galileo* (1937–9) or *Mother Courage* (1941), Brecht was much less didactic, and much more sensitive and sympathetic in shaping his own characters.

In 1941, while waiting in Finland for a visa for the United States, he wrote another parable play on Nazism: *The Resistible Rise of Arturo Ui*.

In order to alert Americans, his prospective hosts, to Hitler's escalating expansion, he transferred Nazi aggressiveness to a milieu familiar to them: the world of Chicago gangsters. Moreover, he updated the dirty tricks of the gangsters by infusing them with the method used by the Nazis in taking advantage of economic crisis to enforce political dictatorship.

In the rhymed Prologue, the 'gangster of the gangsters', Arturo Ui, is compared to Richard III, and the play itself reveals many more Shakespearian features. A parody of Elizabethan heroic blank verse is employed in alienating and ridiculing the speeches of contemporary businessmen and gunmen. Arturo Ui himself hires an old, out-at-elbows actor to teach him how to walk, stand, sit, and speak in the grand style of Shakespeare's heroes. The most convenient model for his demagogic oratory is found in Mark Antony's funeral oration over Caesar's corpse. Later on, Ui accosts Betty Dullfeet at the funeral of her husband Ignatius Dullfeet, councillor and newspaper publisher in Chicago's suburb Cicero, whose death he had ordered; his impudent harassment is modelled on Richard III's wooing of Lady Anne over the coffin of Henry VI, her father-in-law, whom he has murdered. The parallel with the Austrian Chancellor Dollfuss, who was assassinated in 1934 on Hitler's command, is stressed by the punning name.

The ghost of another victim of Ui appearing to him in a horrible dream recalls Shakespeare's procession of ghosts frightening Richard III before the battle of Bosworth. In the ending, Ui, supported by the long-resisting widow of Dullfeet, is shown in full command of the citizens of Chicago and Cicero, while many other American cities are asking for his 'protection'. The similarity with terrorized Austria after Hitler's 'friendly' annexation (*Anschluss*) in 1938 could not be missed.

In making Ui both a ridiculous and a horrifying figure, Brecht relied on centuries-old theatre experience, going back to medieval mysteries and moralities and proving that audiences could be both amused and repelled by attractive stage villains. The medieval Vice, Shakespeare's Richard III, and Brecht's shameless Nazi gangster Ui can shake hands as prominent examples of such a double effect. One of the most Brechtian lines of the whole play is given to a bloodstained Woman, representing common humanity and addressing all decent people:

Where are you? Help! Will no one stop this plague?

To Brecht's disappointment, *The Resistible Rise of Arturo Ui* was not produced in the United States during his exile there. In 1947, he was investigated by the Un-American Activities Committee, and decided to return to Europe. After an intensely creative but relatively quiet stay in Switzerland, he settled in East Berlin, the most allergic part of the Soviet bloc, where in 1949 he and his collaborators founded a dynamic theatre company, the Berliner Ensemble.

In 1951–2 Brecht launched into his most daring Shakespearian venture: a basic adaptation of *Coriolanus*. Using two English editions, the classic German translation by Dorothea Tieck, and the ancient historical works by Plutarch and Livy, he reshaped Shakespeare by consistently downgrading Coriolanus and upgrading the Roman citizens and their tribunes. He also updated the historical events by sophisticated touches which did not deny Shakespeare's representation of the early Roman republic controlled by rich patricians but infused it with his own historical perspective and world-view. He wanted to show that the proud and arrogant aristocratic warrior had to finish up in democratic Rome as an obsolete obstacle to peaceful life. In form, he preserved Shakespeare's five-act structure and the scene-division usual in modern editions, only cutting the scenes to make them shorter and more terse. Great care was given to the opening scene of the plebeians' insurrection, which was discussed by Brecht and three of his collaborators in a dialogue written down in 1963 in preparation for rehearsals. Answering the question whether it is proper to change Shakespeare, Brecht quipped: 'I think we can change Shakespeare if we *can* change him' (that is, if we know how to do it).

In his changed version, he introduced the riotous citizens as better organized and more resolute than they are in Shakespeare. Brecht's plebeians carry knives besides staves and clubs and ask not only for bread at their own price but also for olives—which, of course, mean better nourishment but also symbolize peace (as in Shakespeare's Sonnet 107 and several of his plays, e.g. *Timon of Athens*, 5.5.87). Brecht was at his best in such small but significant hints in which his materialistic view was enhanced by his poetic vision. To make the opposition between peace and war fully resonant, the First Citizen immediately contrasts the 'olives' with the threat of Coriolanus' 'armed violence'. The plebeians are resolved to kill Coriolanus as their chief enemy because he mocks at their demands. Their desperate plight is stressed by the addition of the Third Citizen who is accompanied by his little son and wants to emigrate from Rome to avoid starving or fighting for the rich. The First Citizen, whose Shakespearian black humour is fully preserved, is sure that a better Rome can be fought out for the boy.

The 'pretty tale' of Shakespeare's compromising, loquacious patrician Menenius is shortened, and attention is centred on Coriolanus: he does not enter alone, as in Shakespeare, but with his armed guard with whom he has just suppressed a corn riot in another part of the city. Soon he has to face, with disgust, two Tribunes who have been conceded by the Senate as the people's representatives. They enter, acclaimed by the citizens, together with two generals and senators who proclaim that war is imminent because the neighbouring Volsci have been informed about the inner strife in Rome and are approaching to attack it. Coriolanus is only too glad to divert the mutineers to a foreign enemy, and Tribune Brutus exhorts them to be 'good fighters for a good Rome'. This is a substantial departure from Shakespeare whose 'Citizens steal away' instead of following Coriolanus. Brecht hated this stage direction and consoled himself and his collaborators with the false idea that all stage directions were added to Shakespeare's texts by other hands.

The scenes of the Roman campaign against the Volscian capital Corioli, and Coriolanus' bravery, for which he is granted his honorary surname (Act 1, Scenes 4–10), were not adapted by Brecht because he wanted to telescope them into one massive scene after they had been put together and tried out in rehearsals; unfortunately, the actual rehearsals started only eight years after his premature death. The rest of the play, however, was adapted by him to the very end, which was given as much attention as the opening. In Brecht's Act 5, the Tribunes organize Roman resistance against a new attack of the Volsci who are led now not only by their general Aufidius but also by Coriolanus himself. From the chief enemy of the people he has turned into a merciless adversary of the whole of Rome after being banished from it by the Tribunes, in the people's name, because he refused to distribute the seized Volscian corn to them. The climactic scene (5.3) in which Shakespeare's Coriolanus yields to the pleas of his mother Volumnia and decides to negotiate peace between the two warring nations takes a sharp turn: Brecht's Volumnia describes to Coriolanus the new Rome in which the people are fully armed and determined to resist his aggression, while Roman patricians are faced with a fatal dilemma—either to be obliged to the rabble for saving Rome from the Volsci or to be obliged to the Volsci for saving the Roman aristocracy from the rabble. When Coriolanus resolves not to attack Rome, Aufidius accuses him of high treason and commands Volscian officers to fall upon him and stab him to death.

In the effort to stress the political conflicts of the play, Brecht blurred the human motives in Coriolanus' behaviour. Shakespeare's proud warrior is moved by his human feelings to conclude peace at the cost of his own life and reaches tragic greatness. Brecht's Coriolanus appears to be both moved by his mother and deterred by the military prowess of the Roman people.

In Brecht no one pays final tribute to Coriolanus' 'noble memory'. Instead, a short scene is added to underscore the irrelevance of the warrior in peaceful Rome. Here Brecht changed not only Shakespeare but also Plutarch, from whom he probably drew the information that Coriolanus' family were permitted by the Senate to wear mourning for ten months. In Brecht's adaptation, Menenius' motion in the Senate to commemorate the hero is interrupted by Tribune Brutus who moves that the Senate proceed with the current agenda: to return the conquered lands to the citizens of Corioli and build an aqueduct from the third hill of Rome to the gardens in the east. The family petition to wear public mourning for Coriolanus is rejected and, in a Brechtian epic ending, the action is left open by a simple stage direction: 'The Senate continues its normal business.'

Probably more than any other Shakespeare play, *Coriolanus* has tended to be involved in current social and political conflicts. It is now generally assumed that Shakespeare's own interest in the story was stimulated by the peasants' insurrection in his native Midlands in 1607. The most notorious political turmoil sparked by the play erupted in Paris in 1933–4 when the production at the Comédie Française was received as a right-wing attack on the socialist government then in power. Less known is the fact that Brecht's preoccupation with *Coriolanus* also coincided, in June 1953, with an unexpected political event: mass demonstrations of East Berlin workers against the government's regulations concerning labour productivity. When the demonstrations grew into demands for the abdication of the government and free elections, they were crushed with Soviet tanks. Immediately,

Brecht wrote letters to the Communist leaders, appealing to them to take the demonstrations as a challenge for serious discussion of labour problems. The Communist bureaucracy pulled their favourite trick: Brecht's appeal was stifled and only the last sentence of his letter, expressing his general support for the socialist state, was published.

The events were dramatized in 1966, with a good deal of poetic licence, by the West German author Günther Grass. In his play, *The Plebeians Rehearse the Uprising*, the rehearsal of the first scene of Brecht's *Coriolanus* is interrupted by news of an uprising of workers, some of whom arrive in the theatre to seek support from the Boss (the Brecht-figure). His reaction, however, is ambiguous, as he is torn between his loyalty to the government and his sympathies with the rebels. In his moment of recognition, he declares: 'We can't change Shakespeare unless we change ourselves.' The new experience calls for a radical revision of both artistic and personal attitudes.

Not until 1964 was Brecht's *Coriolanus* staged by his Berliner Ensemble, and in the following year it toured to London and Prague. The two directors, Manfred Wekwerth and Joachim Tenschert, re-adapted Brecht's adaptation, restoring some of Shakespeare's original features, such as the strong dependence of Coriolanus upon his patrician mother. Their own invention and precision was best shown in the scenes of the battle of Corioli, left unadapted by Brecht. Their soldiers clashed in the stylized manner of Peking opera, and Coriolanus fought Aufidius in single combat grinning like a samurai delighting in his professional skill. The insanity of warring stood out with forceful effect. The set was a monumental city gate on a revolve, chalk white on one side for Rome and roughly timbered on the other for Corioli, turning like Coriolanus himself.

Much acclaimed in London in 1965, this visit of the Berliner Ensemble was not the first. As early as 1956, they had come to perform Brecht's own play *The Caucasian Chalk Circle* and started a whole period of Brechtian influence in England, consolidating the impact they had made in Paris in 1954. Brecht's last advice to his actors before they went to London, pinned to the notice board in his theatre just nine days before his untimely death, pointed out two things to be borne in mind: 'First: we shall be offering most of the audience a pure pantomime, a kind of silent film on the stage, for they know no German... Second: there is in England a long-standing fear that German art (literature, painting, music) must be terribly heavy, slow, laborious, pedestrian. So our playing needs to be quick, light, strong."[18]

This was Brecht's touching as well as pertinent farewell to his actors. Their visits to London can be seen as a reciprocation of the first tours of the English Comedians to the Continent. Then as now, the actors could not be understood easily by the audiences and had to rely on their skilled physical action; nevertheless, their impact was strong and long-lasting. The Berliner Ensemble's guest productions of *The Caucasian Chalk Circle* and *Coriolanus* in London brought the cultural exchange between England and the Continent full circle. It is worth noticing that both in the old days and in our own time Shakespeare's share in the exchange was very important.

Brecht's impact on English theatre could be felt in the cruder, sparser, and more socially engaged modes of directing, acting, staging, and playwriting, even though some theatre companies were attracted more by Brecht's style, inspired by the forceful simplicity of the Elizabethan stage, than by his political message. In East Germany, Brecht's authority was so great that it reinforced Marxist interpretations of Shakespeare in both criticism and directing. On the other hand, it encouraged East German directors, critics, and scholars to be experimental, enquiring, and inventive. Probably the best representatives of the Brechtian heritage were the French Swiss Beno Besson, Brecht's disciple and most creative successor, and Robert Weimann, East Germany's most important theoretician.

A good example of Besson's experimental directing was the production of *Hamlet* at the Volksbühne (People's Theatre) in East Berlin in 1977, also staged in the same year in French at Avignon and later in Belgium. It denied the streamlined constructs of hard-line Marxist-Leninists by not presenting Hamlet as a noble intellectual born before the right time of socialist humanism, but as a robust, boorish, contradictory character whose clownish tomfoolery or even ruthless brutality were his forms of reaction against the brutal world around him. His Freudian mother fixation provocatively deviated from the current tenets of socialist realism. Altogether, private relationships seemed to be given more prominence than social and political concerns. The bare stage, surrounded by grey rectangular screens and streaked by long shadows cast by the front lighting, created an atmosphere of a menacing labyrinth in which the perplexity and inscrutability of personal and social relations were reflected.

Critics noticed that Manfred Karge's Hamlet reacted for the most part intelligently, sometimes courageously, but at other times elusively. Similar contradictions were apparent in his temper, sometimes jovial to the point of farce, sometimes serious to the point of frustration and despair. His monologues were quiet, reflective, and analytical but suddenly they would burst into high theatricality. After the play-within-the-play, he pranced about dressed up as a king in a satin robe but his crown was of paper. Although no kinship with Vysotsky's contemporary Hamlet at Moscow's Taganka Theatre was noticeable, there was a similarity to the grotesque Moscow Hamlet of 1932 who also paraded with a paper crown on his head.

Besson's iconoclastic direction reached its climax in the ending, when neither Hamlet nor Fortinbras appeared as the White Princes of the neo-Romantic Marxist interpretation, as precursors of a socialist future. To shock the audience, the part of Fortinbras was given to Beno Besson's 10-year-old son Pierre whose final 'Bid the soliders shoot' could not possibly mean a highly respectable military salute to the dead hero. It rather signalled a new round of infantile violence.

This *Hamlet* can be considered as a creative development of Brecht's views, expressed in his working diary and one of his sonnets: Hamlet's doubts about taking revenge were perfectly reasonable at a time when revenge, ennobled by Greek tragedy, was ruled out by Christianity; but the encounter with Fortinbras's army of fools stirred him up to unreasonable 'heroic' action and the horrible final bloodshed.[19]

More immediately, Besson's *Hamlet* was inspired and, after its staging, defended by Robert Weimann whose constant questioning of traditional ideas about culture, literature, and drama was opening new approaches to Shakespeare. One of Weimann's main lines of research started from Brecht's argument that modern productions of Shakespeare's plays should be based on the knowledge of the stage for which they were written. To provide such knowledge as thoroughly as possible, Weimann explored the prehistoric origins of drama in cults and rituals and then proceeded to enquire into the social function of dramatic form and language in ancient Greek and Roman tragedies and comedies, late medieval English mysteries and moralities, as well as folk plays and customs. His book *Shakespeare and the Popular Tradition in the Theatre* (German edn. East Berlin, 1967; English edn., revised and updated, Baltimore, 1978) stressed popular dramatic and verbal elements in Shakespeare's plays, such as the mixture of seriousness and farce, sense and nonsense, matter and impertinency, rule and misrule, authority and its inversion in topsy-turvydom. Like many other Marxist scholars, Weimann tended to overestimate the creative role of the working classes in the production of both material goods and social entertainment. It is also true that his attempts at connecting prehistoric cults and rituals with the late medieval and early Renaissance dramatic form were based on a good deal of unprovable speculation. But his close examination of the Elizabethan stage in all its different areas and levels and in their relation to the audience, as well as his sophisticated analyses of such ambivalent figures as the Vice or the Fool and his successors (including Pickleherring), offered much deeper understanding of Shakespeare's stage and of the disparate sources that nourished his plays.

In revealing the popular tradition in Shakespeare's theatre Weimann did not ignore the importance of non-popular sources, especially the erudite humanist and Renaissance literature and drama. He saw Shakespeare's greatest achievement in the synthesis of both popular and highly cultivated traditions creating the inexhaustible vitality and artistic value of English national drama. He was also convinced that our reception of Shakespeare should integrate Goethe's enlightened poetic insight with Brecht's non-illusionistic epic alienation.

Weimann's later books, essays, and reviews discussed Shakespeare's plays as rich in both plebeian and aristocratic stances and other contradictions, dramatic paradoxes, ironies, and ambiguities, posing many unresolved problems that could be clarified only by advanced international theory admitting of plurality of approaches. His profound analysis of the crisis of authority in late Elizabethan England and its representation in Shakespearian theatre encouraged thoughtful questioning of any authority at any time. Although he occasionally came under fire from both hard-line Marxists at home and traditional scholars in the West, his contribution to cultural theory and stage practice has had an undeniably liberating effect.

The 1980s were marked, in East Germany and all over the Soviet bloc, by a growing dissatisfaction with the immobile and increasingly senile Communist leadership and by the attempts of more enlightened and far-sighted Communists at a radical reconstruction of the whole society. Mikhail Gorbachev's perestroika, reviving the stifled initiative of the Prague Spring and calling for a far-reaching political, economic, and social democratization, was anticipated and supported by liberating cultural trends, including some critical interpretations and productions of Shakespeare, as we have just noticed. To give one more example from another genre, *Love's Labour's Lost*, produced at the Prague National Theatre in 1987, was subtly subversive in many aspects, starting with postmodern action sets which were centred round the ornate nineteenth-century safety curtain. In Czech, as in Russian, the safety curtain is traditionally called 'iron curtain', so that it offered, in the new political situation, an irresistible visual metaphor. Mischievously, it descended and ascended several times during the performance, at one time stopping just a few inches above the stage floor, leaving the actor only a thin gap to finish his speech as if from behind the Iron Curtain. The oppressive nature of the Academy of the King of Navarre, prescribing a three-year plan of chastity and pure scholarship, was foregrounded by the three lords of Navarre slamming their clenched fists against the iron curtain as they took their oaths. The hollow sound of the curtain indicated the hollowness and stupidity of their dogmatic resolve.[20]

The greatest fun, however, was reached with all the four gentlemen of Navarre wooing the Princess of France and her three ladies in waiting by performing their Russian masque (5.2). During the preceding production of *Love's Labour's Lost* in Prague in 1970, shortly after the Soviet-led invasion had frozen the Prague Spring, the Russian wooers had to be changed into Persians, even though well-informed spectators knew what the scene was really about. Now in 1987, when the long Soviet occupation was loosening its grip, the lords, 'disguised as Russians' in huge fur caps, furiously parodied a Cossack dance. Their assurance that they wanted 'Nothing but peace and gentle visitation' was laughed at bitterly, and liberating bursts of laughter were triggered when the Princess of France took her merry leave of the unwelcome suitors: 'Twenty adieus, my frozen Muscovites' and when a little later she declared with equal joyfulness: 'A mess of Russians left us but of late.' Czech audiences were only too eager to embrace a happy vision that still seemed remote in real life.

Probably the most subversive Shakespeare production in the years immediately preceding the collapse of the totalitarian regimes, including the Berlin Wall and the Iron Curtain, was the Romanian *Hamlet* directed by Alexandru Tocilescu in Bucharest. It played for over 200 performances to packed houses before the overthrow and execution of the Communist dictator Nicolae Ceauşescu in 1989; in September 1990, it was revived at the Royal National Theatre in London.

Like the Polish *Hamlet* of 1956, it brimmed over with topical political allusions, extending from touches of bitter irony to whole scenes of spying, scheming, and sudden deaths. The irony started very early in the play, as the common soldiers at Elsinore castle complained about 'the bitter cold' during their night watch while the actual watchers of the production had to sit in unheated houses. The severe economic cuts of Ceauşescu, notorious for his lavish lifestyle, were ridiculed more extensively when Hamlet explained why his mother's new wedding followed 'hard upon' his father's funeral: 'Thrift, thrift, Horatio. The funeral baked meats | Did coldly furnish forth the marriage tables' (1.2.179–80). Since the Romanian word for 'thrift' is 'economia', which was exactly the term used by the Communist government to cover all sorts of austerity measures, the audiences were bursting with both laughter and indignation. Much more seriously and threateningly, the Ghost of Hamlet's father did not appear, and the spectators could only hear his terrifying voice accompanied by two searchlights sweeping the stage and crossing each other in a scenic metaphor of the search for all those who tried to cross the Iron Curtain.

Ion Caramitru's Hamlet was trapped within this prison, exposed to espionage and interrogation; during his soliloquies, he sat rigidly in a chair, constricted and constrained, under cruel, piercing light.[21] As in Besson's *Hamlet*, the attraction between his mother and himself was revealed as a love–hate affair. The most daring innovations were introduced in the ending: Horatio, the only upright supporter of Hamlet's fight against tyranny and search for truth, was not given the privilege of defending his friend's 'wounded name' by telling the whole story of 'cruel, bloody, and unnatural acts'. Instead, he was stabbed to death by Fortinbras's personal guards. Fortinbras himself arrived as a new military dictator in red uniform, surrounded by his secret agents led by Rosencrantz and Guildenstern, who had not been put to death in England. With a vengeance, they returned to fortify the new regime of oppression and deceit. The dangers of the immediate political developments in Romania and some other parts of Eastern Europe were foreshadowed with a most alarming anticipation and urgent warning.

FURTHER READING

Jan Kott's essays *Shakespeare our Contemporary* were published in English in 1964 separately in London and New York and have been reprinted many times. Two books by Grigori Kozintsev appeared in English as *Shakespeare: Time and Conscience* (New York, 1966) and *King Lear: The Space of Tragedy* (Berkeley and Los Angeles, 1977). The best criticism of Kozintsev's films *Hamlet* and *King Lear* can be found in Anthony Davies and Stanley Wells (eds.), *Shakespeare and the Moving Image* (Cambridge, 1994). Kozintsev's film *King Lear* is now also on cassette by Hollywood's Attic, 1996, and Tartan Video, 1997. Innovative Shakespeare productions in Moscow, Prague, and East Germany are discussed, in broad international context, in Dennis Kennedy (ed.), *Foreign Shakespeare* (Cambridge, 1993). Robert Weimann's essay 'Shakespeare on the Modern Stage: Past Significance and Present Meaning', *Shakespeare Survey*, 20 (1967), is a good introduction to his theoretical thought. Translator, critic, and editor Maik Hamburger has used his rich theatrical experience in his essay on 'Consolidation and Subversion in East German Shakespeare productions from 1945 to about 1970', *Shakespeare Survey*, 48 (1995). He has also contributed a separate section on the theatres of the former German Democratic Republic to Wilhelm Hortmann's valuable *Shakespeare on the German Stage*, ii: *1914– 1990* (Cambridge, 1998). Manfred Pfister's admirably balanced essay 'Hamlets Made in Germany, East and West' is in Michael Hattaway, Boika Sokolova, and Derek Roper (eds.), *Shakespeare in the New Europe* (Sheffield, 1994). Precise summaries and evaluations of modern Shakespearian adaptations and transformations in English, French, and German are provided by Ruby Cohn in *Modern Shakespeare Offshoots* (Princeton, 1976). A selection of Eastern and Central European Studies *Shakespeare and his Contemporaries* was edited by Jerzy Limon and Jay L. Halio (Newark, Del., 1993).

6

Post-Communist Shakespeare

The collapse of totalitarian regimes in Eastern Europe by the end of 1989 took very different courses, from the shortest and the merriest 'velvet revolution' in Czechoslovakia to the hasty political trials and ghastly televised executions of the Communist dictator and his wife in Romania. A peaceful separation between Slovakia and the Czech Republic had its counterpart in the furious nationalist wars, ethnic cleansings, atrocious racial rapes, and massacres in the Balkans.

As to theatres, they have been liberated from oppressive political control; their freedom, however, has been exposed to the pressures of the free market. Actors, who were often, along with students, the driving force in toppling Communist governments, barbed-wire fences, and walls, have to face new problems and to look for sponsors, because state and municipal subsidies of arts are much smaller than they used to be. Some theatres have been closed down; new theatres are opening, trying hard to make ends meet and to achieve both economic and artistic success. Since Shakespeare knew best how to do it, his plays still attract audiences in spite of the flood of commercial culture or subculture prevailing in the TV and film entertainment industry. He offers theatre-goers such mystery and action thrillers as *Hamlet* or *Macbeth*, such love stories as *Romeo and Juliet*, *Twelfth Night*, or *Othello*, and such romances as *The Tempest*, *The Winter's Tale*, *Cymbeline*, or *Pericles*. Much more than that, he continues to hold his mirror up to nature, society, and each individual.

Mirrors were certainly prominent in the Cracow *Hamlet* directed and designed in 1989 by the distinguished Polish man of the theatre and film Andrzej Wajda (his previous productions of the tragedy were premièred in 1960 and twice in 1981). His *Hamlet IV* straddled the East European revolutions and attracted international attention by guest performances in the United States, Mexico, Italy, Israel, Austria, Japan, and Germany. Wajda's chief inspiration was not so much Jan Kott as the symbolist artist, writer, and director Stanisław Wyspiański whom we noticed before as a daring visionary of Hamlet's incessant search for truth. The intricacy of truth was symbolized by a whole array of mirrors placed at strategic positions and angles, the most prominent of them standing on Hamlet's dressing table and facing the audience.

To draw the audience into the search for truth, Wajda gave them the privilege of sitting with Hamlet in a small, intimate group at the back of the stage, set up as the actor's green-room. All the rest of the stage, seen only partly by Hamlet and the spectators, was occupied by the other characters in their play of power and vanity, with the dark and empty auditorium in the background. Some of the characters came to speak to Hamlet at the entrance to the green-room. The intimacy and emotional charge of the occasion were heightened by the fine actress Teresa Budzisz-Krzyżanowska who took the part of the Prince (another female Hamlet appeared simultaneously in a German production in East Berlin). In the process of her acting, especially in her soliloquies, she was intent on revealing her own identity as well as that of Hamlet, encouraging the audience to participate in the exploration and include themselves in it.

Like Besson's German *Hamlet* in 1977, Wajda's *Hamlet IV* concentrated on personal, psychological probing, leaving larger social issues mostly aside. Whereas his first *Hamlet* was replete with political allusions, culminating in the presentation of Fortinbras as a Soviet military commander, in his *Hamlet IV* Fortinbras entered into dead Hamlet's sanctuary to take over his/her role. On the stage, a restored Claudius figure started to repeat the pompous succession speech (1.2), while Fortinbras looked at the vanity fair from his inner room with sadness and contempt.

Wajda did not pretend to know more than Hamlet in his/her groping for truth. Avoiding any ideological patterns, the production, like Shakespeare's tragedy, did not give definite answers to what was the ultimate truth. Less assertively but more rewardingly, it endowed the spectators with a wealth of feelings, thoughts, and suggestions about what was true and what was false in both art and life.

As if by contrast, a monumental *Hamlet* was introduced in March 1990 at the Deutsches Theater (German Theatre) of what was still East Berlin, the capital of the German Democratic Republic (six months later, Germany was reunited). It was directed by another disciple of Bertolt Brecht, the playwright and Shakespearian translator and adapter Heiner Müller, author of two Shakespeare offshoots: *Macbeth* (1971) and *Hamletmaschine* (1977). The latter is a short play and pantomime of five extremely baffling, provocative scenes, projecting the story of Hamlet into the twentieth century, when the socialist dreams of several European generations are dashed by cruelty and terror: 'Something is rotten in this Age of Hope.' Müller's text combines the devices of parody, grotesque, and the theatre of cruelty in a montage of allusions not only to *Hamlet* but also to *Richard III*, *Macbeth*, and many other canonical works. The totally disillusioned actor doing Hamlet refuses to play any more roles and, during an anti-Communist insurrection, is swayed by divided loyalties between the rebels and the defenders of the state. He wants to become a machine without pain and thought. Finally, however, he puts on the armour of the Ghost representing 'the beloved blood-thirsty dog' (Stalin) and splits the busts of Marx, Lenin, and Mao, throwing the world back into the Ice Age. Ophelia, after her metamorphosis from an aggressive anarchist into a whore performing striptease, is lashed to a wheelchair in the final scene and, all in white, as an avenging Electra, declares her intention to reject the world she had given birth to, invoking 'hatred, contempt, rebellion, death'. In the world where machines have taken control of human beings, violence breaks out as a spasm of oppressed humanity.

Müller's iconoclastic montage was first published only in West Germany and was dismissed by most East German critics as pornographic, anti-humanist, and decadent. In 1990, however, Müller inserted it into his translation of *Hamlet*, creating a huge sandwich play which lasted seven and a half hours and was called *Hamlet/ Maschine*. The spectators were overwhelmed by colossal eclectic sets centred in a massive concrete shelter, alluding visually to the incarcerated but sheltered life in East Germany. The opening action was encased in a stage-high gauze screen which represented a big block of ice slowly melting and producing the sound of a constant trickle of water and a large puddle in the middle of the stage: a scenographic metaphor of the Soviet bloc with its thaws and final dissolution. The ominous Ghost stalked across the stage as a naked king with only his helmet and a codpiece left, while a muted radio broadcast of Stalin's funeral evoked his mass murders, still haunting the world.

Most of the action was presented in slow, ritual style, alleviated by light Brechtian touches of sarcastic humour and irony. Hamlet was a slim, sensitive young intellectual wearing a double-breasted black suit, too large for him, as was his task to set right the disjointed time. The second part of the action was located in a monumental tunnel through time, connecting a stately Renaissance architecture upstage with a huge underground tube downstage. In the final scenes, an expanse of reddish sand was planted with bright metal sheets of multiple connotations: they were mirrors, of course, but perhaps also heat collectors, causing the accelerated end of the world, and they were used as tombstones on which the dying characters wrote their names. The dead body of Hamlet, hanging over the stage front, was lovingly taken up and carried onto the stage by Ophelia who repeated the final lines of Electra from *Hamletmaschine* before she was consumed by a blazing fire. Fortinbras entered, wearing a golden helmet combined with a business suit, and covered Hamlet's face with a gilded business folder—obviously hinting at Chancellor Kohl with the almighty German Mark. Over the loudspeaker, the deeply ironic 'Elegy of Fortinbras' by the contemporary Polish poet Zbigniew Herbert was recited, stating bluntly that Hamlet had to perish because he was not for life but chased chimeras and believed 'in crystal notions, not in human clay'; with shocking pragmatism, Fortinbras delineated his immediate tasks: a sewer project, a decree on prostitutes and beggars, and, most alarmingly, 'a better system of prisons'. His intention was 'to take the city by the neck and shake it a bit'.

Müller's *Hamlet/Maschine* could be received as a farewell to the Communist era in East Germany, as perhaps the crowning Shakespearian production of a collapsed social order, and, finally, as a warning vision of the brave new world. It was an artistic obituary stemming from the director's conviction that the German Democratic Republic was not so bad that it did not deserve a decent funeral.

In the rest of the former Communist empire, some directors who had won recognition during their exiles in the West have returned for good or for long stays at their home theatres. In 1991, two outstanding

Romanian directors, Liviu Ciulei and Andrei Serban, revitalized their successful American productions of *A Midsummer Night's Dream* and *Twelfth Night* with profuse topical allusions to the new situation in Bucharest. A special case in point was Malvolio in Serban's *Twelfth Night*, showing unmistakable features of a former Communist cadre, still clinging to the old dogmatic ways of thought and opposing new freedom and abandon. (A similar Malvolio had strutted upon Czech stages in the 1980s.) His final threat 'I'll be revenged on the whole pack of you' was enlarged by just one word: 'hoodlums'. Yet this single word was acutely relevant to what was happening outside the theatre, in University Square, where in the spring of 1991 young people were meeting in 'a zone free from Communism'. At that time the main political power was still held by former, less discredited Communists who repeatedly branded the protesting, singing youth as 'hoodlums'. Malvolio's costume in the scene of his incarceration for lunacy, striped prison wear, identified him with the members of the former Party Central Committee during their imprisonment and hearings in law courts, televised for millions of agonized Romanians. The farcical interrogation of Malvolio by the fool Feste offered a welcome relief from the agony.

In neighbouring Bulgaria, comedies also prevailed in 1992, and their accents were bitter and sarcastic in different ways, referring to the nationwide debate on Communist guilt and democratic retribution. When the ending of *Much Ado about Nothing* was extended by the much abused Hero declaring ironically 'Nobody is guilty', audiences responded with the pleasure and shock of recognition. The general mood of sarcasm among all the hustle and bustle of accommodation in the tempestuous new world reached its most striking and sophisticated expression in *The Tempest*. The highly ambiguous magus Prospero, clad in a black ragged gown, appeared as a slick old manipulator who was content to dismiss both Miranda and her alter ego Ariel (played by the same actress) into thin air and pronounce his epilogue of mercy and forgiveness in the most unromantic, grumbling, and stammering manner.

The fear of manipulation intruding into the spirit of new freedom and experiment was felt acutely also in *Romeo and Juliet*, which had been the most popular Shakespeare play in Bulgaria since the nine-teenth century. Beginning in 1991 at the Student Centre in Sofia, it was drastically shortened but, on the other hand, enlarged and enlivened by fast-moving pantomime in which dummies were used as the main props. They were dismembered and assembled again by the actors until they seemed to be equal partners of Romeo and Juliet who merged with them so intimately that they themselves finally looked like dummies, like grotesque counterparts to the menacing machines of Heiner Müller. Verbal communication was mostly replaced by body language. Free speech and free love were metamorphosed into an absurdist play-cum-pantomime, ending, or rather stopping, with Juliet's puzzled 'Why?' Surviving the tragedy, she wondered why she was drawn into all the chaos.

A totally different, profoundly tragic *Romeo and Juliet* originated not far from Sofia, in the Macedonian capital Skopje, where a Romany (Gypsy) company called Pralipe (Brotherhood) was founded in the 1980s. Directed by the Romany poet Rahim Burhan and inspired by Artaud's theatre of cruelty, they started to include Shakespeare in their repertoire from 1988 (*Macbeth*, *Othello*). In 1991, they had to leave their country and ask for political and cultural asylum in Germany (Mül-heim, Theatre-upon-Ruhr), also touring many other parts of Europe (Vienna, Prague, Brno).

Their action-packed *Romeo and Juliet* (premièred 1994) concen-trated on the central theme of death-marked love, updated by the 'new mutiny', the new outburst of violence in the nationalist war in Bosnia-Herzegovina. Fair Verona was moved to the ancient city of Mostar with its famous mountain bridge which had been built by the Turks on the important trade route from Europe to Asia but was destroyed in 1992. The bombed-out bridge was represented by a battered steel construction, forming Juliet's terrifying balcony on one side of the gorge; the separated lovers were forced to voice their desperate desire across the abyss. Despite all the dreadful obstacles, Muslim Juliet and Christian Romeo celebrated their secret wedding night in a characteristically Romany way: Romeo picked single grapes from a vine and put them into Juliet's mouth so that they could eat the grapes and kiss at the same time. Another simple but forceful device was Romeo's gesture after he had received the news of Juliet's assumed death and bought poison to commit suicide: he threw heaps of the remaining ducats all around him in a gesture of defiance. When he broke into Juliet's tomb, he raised her alleged corpse high in the air and danced with it furiously, as if feeling against all reason that he might bring her back to life.

After the tragic deaths of the young lovers, there was no reconciliation between the fatal foes, no glooming peace announced in this Bosnian tragedy. Only more bursts of gunfire alarmed the spectators to the full realization of the madness of military arrogance, causing endless suffering, despair, and death among civilians. In a breathtaking performance lasting ninety minutes without interval, the Romany Brotherhood created a unique intercultural event, a forceful succession to the crude performance of *Romeo and Juliet* by the English Comedians who toured Europe while it was torn apart by the Thirty Years War.[1]

Another dramatic outcry against the fate of young people drawn into a nationalist war was staged in Zagreb in 1992, when the short open war between Croatia and Yugoslavia was formally ended and Croatia's independence was recognized by most European states, but Serbian and Croatian generals were still battling for possession of large parts of Bosnia-Herzegovina. The desperate situation called for desperate responses, and the choice fell on Shakespeare's *Titus Andronicus* to be produced for the first time ever by a Croatian company. It was not, however, the first production of the play in Zagreb; the director Nenni Delmestre acknowledged her indebtedness to Peter Brook's *Titus Andronicus* brought as a guest performance to the Croatian National Theatre in 1957 (when it made a similarly profound impression in Warsaw, as mentioned above).

This time, the play was staged in a long-disused, dilapidated building at the back of the former trade-fair grounds, bleak and poorly lit. The sets were equally bleak and crude: a circular wooden stage with a tall, rough-hewn frame (a ladder, a rack, a cross, or all of them together?) and a pit beneath, in which the many victims of atrocities disappeared. The naturalism and sensationalism of Shakespeare's early tragedy was subdued, and significant changes were introduced into his text to foreground the sacrifice of youth in war. Most surprisingly and daringly, the Roman general Titus was presented as a young man, his sons were changed into his brothers and his daughter Lavinia into his sister, all wearing eclectic modern costumes with allusions to Heavy Metal and the films *A Clockwork Orange* and *Mad Max*.

The contemporary relevance of the production was best described by the director herself stating in the programme note that their *Titus* aimed to be a play about Croatia, about the horrors of its war and post-war times, about an enormous wound which had no chance of healing as it grew deeper instead, becoming a grave in which all hope for justice and life worth living were buried.[2] Although the horrors of the Bosnian conflict provoked strong responses in Shakespeare productions in other parts of Europe, including Germany and Britain, the Croatian *Titus* and the Romany *Romeo and Juliet* have to be considered as, so far, the most authentic artistic reflections on the third Balkan War.

Irresistibly, *King Lear*, with its theme of the division of both kingdom and family and its tortuous complexities, attracted Eastern Europe while the world of Communism was crumbling away. In the West, the shift of interest from *Hamlet* to *King Lear* as Shakespeare's central play, seen no more as a tragedy of redemption but as one of despair, has been noticed since the 1960s.[3] In the East, the position of *Hamlet* has been so strong that fully resonant productions of *King Lear* have been much slower in asserting themselves. Although Count Tolstoy's totally negative criticism of the tragedy was never fully accepted, it took such great achievements as Kozintsev's film to draw the attention of large audiences.

In a very independent, very Georgian way, the theatre director Robert Sturua (whose *Richard III* was discussed above) surprised spectators and critics both at home and in the West, including the United States, by producing *King Lear* (from 1987 onwards) with far-reaching political overtones. He presented the King as a cunning dictator hiding behind the mask of a benign patriarchal ruler. The hypnotizing Ramaz Chkhikvadze in the title role first revealed the King's inward nature when he furiously attacked Cordelia for refusing to play the game of flattery and high politics, tore at her clothes, and threw her down to the ground. Most shockingly, he killed the Fool with a knife for mocking him. In the final scenes, he was denied the blessing of death and had to witness the results of his tyranny: alone on stage, he dragged the corpse of his truthful Cordelia behind him, while the world he had deformed collapsed in crashes of a huge, possibly nuclear, explosion.

The killing of the Fool by Lear was enacted also in Hungary, where the tragedy, after two decades of neglect in the 1970s and 1980s, has been revived with remarkable insistency since 1989. The Fool's death at the hands of mad Lear startled Budapest in 1991 at the Madách Theatre (named after a renowned dramatist of the Hungarian National Revival of the nineteenth century). It is probable that both the Hungarian and the Georgian stagings were inspired by Adrian Noble's *King Lear* produced in 1982 at Stratford-upon-Avon, where the striking circus Fool of Antony Sher was stabbed to death by the mad Lear. The inspiration was used more effectively by Sturua, whereas the madness of the Hungarian Lear ended, at least for one critic, in a 'sentimental gush'.

Some remarkable *Lears* have been staged recently in the Czech Republic, but probably the most memorable post-Communist production of the tragedy took place in Moscow in 1992. In fact, there were two *Lears* played in Moscow at that time for several years, but young Sergei Zhenovach's direction at the Malaya Bronnaya Theatre was more profound and rewarding. Like Wajda's *Hamlet IV*, Zhenovach's *Lear* was performed for a small audience (less than 100) seated on the stage, sharing it with actors, while the auditorium was left empty, creating an impression of a vacuum characteristic of the Russian artistic and political situation of the period. All sound effects were excluded, even during the storm. The set was simple to the utmost: just four carved oak beams making a square, marking the framework of a house and indicating that the central concern of the play was with a family losing its home as well as with the tense family relationships that still kept the world together. In his subdued Chekhovian style, the director refused other spectacular effects, so that the Fool almost tiptoed off the stage to be seen no more.

A crucial role in the spiritual revival and integration of both family and society was given to the young generation, especially the self-sacrificing Cordelia and the surviving Edgar, as in Kozintsev's film. This time, however, the final lines of the play were spoken, in accordance with the Quarto version, by the Duke of Albany, who recognized 'the weight of this sad time' but left some hope for young individuals such as Edgar, with his experience of living outside the acquisitive society, in close rapport with nature and the uncorrupted poor. Ecological reverberations were in the air.[4]

Hamlet still holds his ground firmly in Eastern Europe, assuming many new shapes, often radically different from the dissident Hamlets of the late stages of the Soviet Empire. He has changed into an anarchistic raving maniac in Sofia, a stammering, endearing epileptic in Prague, an aggressive though completely confused punk played by a rock star in Lithuania and on tour. In Gdańsk (beginning 1996) they had a ruthless, power-hungry Hamlet without the Ghost but with the absurdist ghost of Jan Kott still going strong. In Moscow, a dark, bloodthirsty Hamlet staged in 1994 without either Ghost or Fortinbras was followed in 1995 by *The Comedy about the Prince of Denmark*, presenting K. S. Stanislavsky in conversation with the Prince. In Tbilisi, now the capital of the Republic of Georgia, another offshoot based on *Hamlet* and Tom Stoppard's *Rosencrantz and Guildenstern Are Dead* was shown in 1996. In the same year, a Serbian adaptation entitled *Hamlet, Comments* enriched the programme of the Yugoslavian Shakespeare Festival in Belgrade and Subotica.

Reports of increasing interest in Shakespeare's comedies, including the late romances, have arrived not only from Romania and Bulgaria, but also from Yugoslavia, Slovakia, Poland, and Russia. *The Tempest*, which has had almost no Russian stage history, made its way to both the European and the Siberian part of the Russian Federation. Possibly the strongest revivals of Shakespeare's romances have taken place in the Czech Republic, with productions of *The Tempest*, *The Winter's Tale*, *Cymbeline*, and *Pericles*. An innovative *Winter's Tale* was directed in 1992 by Jan Kačer, who was disgraced by the hard-line Communists for his resistance to the Soviet invasion in 1968 but managed, step by step, to conjure up excellent productions of *A Midsummer Night's Dream*, *Twelfth Night*, and *The Tempest* in the provinces or in small off-centre theatres in Prague. After the 'velvet revolution' of 1989, in which he took an active part, he was able to start experimenting with distinguished actors on the large stages of the Prague National Theatre but he remained true to his artistic principles. The most characteristic of them has always been his high respect for Shakespeare's text used as a firm basis for his creative stage interpretations. In this effort, he has received full support from the new translations of Martin Hilský, whose painstaking scholarship is combined with his capacity to draw on all the resources of modern Czech in finding equivalents for both Shakespeare's poetry and his humorously colloquial prose.

That was one of the reasons why the production of *The Winter's Tale* reached its happiest moments in the pastoral Bohemian scenes, in which Autolycus, with a pinch of textual and theatrical updating, stole most of the show. Addressing the audience directly with 'my revenue is the silly cheat' (4.3.27) or 'Ha, ha! What a fool honesty is' (4.4.396) or 'I see this is the time that the unjust man doth thrive' (4.4.674–5), he reminded us, in comic mode, of the old totalitarian days, when Shakespeare stood up as a supreme judge to the abuses of the time. How Shakespeare could possibly divine the cheating tricks of present-day Prague taxi drivers and headwaiters or the much more harmful financial frauds of reckless arrivistes will remain one of his secrets.

On the serious side, the themes of resurrection, restoration, and expiation of crimes were treated with thoughtful consciousness. The resurrected Hermione shocked many spectators when she vigorously slapped King Leontes in the face before forgiving him. The whole production reflected on the miracle of the recent revolution and the pitfalls of the post-revolutionary period. Viewed in the long historical perspective, Autolycus could be seen as a modern successor of Pickle-herring, making direct contact with his spectators through topical allusions to sensational local events.

The prospects for the young generation, repeatedly opened by Shakespeare in the endings of his late plays, have probably contributed to his lasting popularity among both the young and the old. Our students and young people in general all over Eastern Europe continue to enjoy him, meeting his challenge to develop their linguistic and aesthetic potential as well as their social awareness.

In most East European countries, Shakespeare's plays and poems are now received with less political alertness: less as a matter of life and death and more as a thing of beauty and truth. As soon, however, as the political situation grows tense and dangerous, as in the Balkans, Shakespeare again becomes a great help in bearing the weight of the sad time.

FURTHER READING

Shakespeare in the New Europe, a volume of essays edited by Michael Hattaway, Boika Sokolova, and Derek Roper (Sheffield, 1994), offers invaluable information and critical discourse; particularly relevant are the essays by Alexander Shurbanov and Boika Sokolova, Marta Gibińska, Martin Hilský, Mark

Sokolyansky, Odette-Irenne Blumenfeld, Evgenia Pancheva, and Janja Ciglar-Žanić. Maik Hamburger's essay '*Hamlet* at World's End: Heiner Müller's Production in East Berlin' is in Tetsuo Kishi, Roger Pringle, and Stanley Wells (eds.), *Shakespeare and Cultural Traditions* (Newark: University of Delaware Press, 1994). A volume of essays *Hamlet East–West*, edited by Marta Gibińska and Jerzy Limon (Gdańsk, 1998), presents stimulating international critical discussion with plenty of material, both historical and recent.

INTRODUCTION

1. *Hamlet* (3.1.71–5). All quotations from Shakespeare follow the text and line numbering of the single-volume *William Shakespeare: The Complete Works*, general eds. Stanley Wells and Gary Taylor (Oxford, 1986).

1. IN THE BEGINNING

1. Both quotations are from Jerzy Limon, *Gentlemen of a Company: English Players in Central and Eastern Europe, 1590–1660* (Cambridge, 1985), 63 and 83.
2. All quotations are from the article by Irene Morris, 'A Hapsburg Letter', *Modern Language Review*, 69 (1974), 12–22.
3. The original manuscripts of Fynes Moryson's huge *Itinerary* are kept in the Bodleian Library and the Library of Corpus Christi College, Oxford. I quote from Limon, *Gentlemen of a Company*, 1–2, modernizing the spelling.
4. See Jerzy Limon, 'Pictorial Evidence for a Possible Replica of the London Fortune Theatre in Gdańsk', *Shakespeare Survey 32* (1979), 189–99 and Limon, *Gentlemen of a Company*, 129–36.
5. Limon, *Gentlemen of a Company*, 105. Limon quotes from P. Mundy, *The Travels... in Europe and Asia*, ed. R. C. Temple, 5 vols. (London, 1907–36), iv. 181–2.
6. See J. M. Manly (ed.), *Specimens of Pre-Shakespearean Drama*, vol. v (Boston, 1897). I am indebted to Pavel Drábek, graduate student of Charles University, for bringing the play to my attention.
7. *The Winter's Tale*, ed. Stephen Orgel (Oxford, 1996), 53.
8. For extracts from the poem in both the German original and English translation see Albert Cohn, *Shakespeare in Germany in the Sixteenth and Seventeenth Centuries* (London 1865; repr. Wiesbaden, 1967), 60. The full version of the lines about the tumbler is in Ernest Brennecke, *Shakespeare in Germany, 1590–1700* (Chicago, 1964), 8.
9. Family archives of the Archbishop of Prague, Cardinal Count Harrach, are preserved in Vienna; a copy is kept in Prague, State Central Archives, collection of copies (Vienna 25.6.1658).
10. The German version and its translation back into English were printed by Cohn, *Shakespeare in Germany*, 309 ff. (quoted here pp. 21–2). A detailed

analysis of the German adaptation can be found in Simon Williams, *Shakespeare on the German Stage*, i: *1586–1914* (Cambridge, 1990), 39–41 and 44.

11. Leslie Hotson, *The Commonwealth and Restoration Stage* (Cambridge, Mass., 1928), 171. The following citations and information about George Jolly also draw on Hotson, pp. 167–76.

2. SHAKESPEARE UNDER THE TSARS

1. A long-standing error should be corrected here. Both Russian and American scholars have spread the notion that in Sumarokov's ending Hamlet marries Ophelia. In fact, no such happy event is mentioned in the finale of Sumarokov's tragedy.

2. E. J. Simmons in his essay 'Catherine the Great and Shakespeare', *Publications of the Modern Language Association of America*, 47 (1932), 790–806, transliterates the name of Mistress Quickly's Russian counterpart as Madame Kela. This is a very odd name for a French go-between. I suspect that there is a word-play in the name which might be transliterated more appropriately as Kiela or Quiela, with an allusion to the French question 'Qui est là?'

3. My chief source for N. M. Karamzin were his *Selected Works* (in Russian, Moscow, 1884) and E. J. Simmons, *English Literature and Culture in Russia 1553–1840* (Cambridge, Mass., 1935).

4. I have drawn chiefly on Russian editions of *Pushkin's Letters* (Moscow, 1926) and Pushkin's *Works* (Moscow, 1949) and on Tatiana A. Wolff's essay 'Shakespeare's Influence on Pushkin's Dramatic Work', *Shakespeare Survey* 5 (1952), 93–105.

5. The English version of Turgenev's paper is available in a paperback volume of essays *Shakespeare in Europe*, ed. Oswald LeWinter (Cleveland, 1963), 171–89. All quotations in this and the following paragraphs are from LeWinter's edition.

6. See Eleanor Rowe, *Hamlet: A Window on Russia* (New York, 1976), 83. I have drawn on this book especially from the chapters 'Dostoevsky and *Hamlet*', '*Hamlet* in the Age of Chekhov and Blok', and 'Pasternak and *Hamlet*'.

7. All quotations from Tolstoy's essay follow the text of LeWinter, *Shakespeare in Europe*, 223–85.

8. *Shaw on Shakespeare*, ed. Edwin Wilson (New York, 1961), 3–5.

9. Nemirovich-Danchenko's reminiscences are reproduced and evaluated by M. Zagorsky in his essay 'Shakespeare in Russia' in G. N. Boyadzhiev, M. B. Zagorsky, and M. M. Morozov (eds.), *Shekspirovsky sbornik 1947* (Shakespeare Miscellany 1947) (Moscow, 1947), 89–95.

10. Konstantin Stanislavsky, *My Life in Art* (New York, 1956), 517. This and the following quotations are from Dennis Kennedy, *Looking at Shakespeare* (Cambridge, 1993), 56. Kennedy includes two sketches and two photographs of Craig's sets for the MAT *Hamlet* on pp. 51–6.

3. SHAKESPEARE AND NATIONAL REVIVALS

1. This and all the following quotations from Polish sources in this chapter draw on Stanisław Helsztyński's essay 'The Fortunes of Shakespeare in Poland', in Stanisław Helsztyński (ed.), *Poland's Homage to Shakespeare* (Warsaw, 1965), 5–33.

2. See András Kiséry, 'Hamletizing the Spirit of the Nation: Political Uses of Kazinczy's 1790 Translation', in Holgar Klein and Péter Dávidházi (eds.), *Shakespeare and Hungary, Shakespeare Yearbook*, vol. 7 (Lewiston, NY, 1996). I am indebted to Kiséry not only for the quotation from Kazinczy's preface but for the whole analysis of the *Hamlet* adaptation.

3. See the journal *Slovenské divadlo* (Slovak Theatre), 12 (1964), 252–78, 423–43, and 28 (1980), 382–407.

4. For the full text of Petőfi's essay see *New Hungarian Quarterly*, 5 (spring 1964), 13 (Shakespeare Memorial Number), 48–51.

4. SHAKESPEARE AFTER THE BOLSHEVIK REVOLUTION

1. Quotations are from Eleanor Rowe, *Hamlet: A Window on Russia* (New York, 1976), 128 and from Vladislav Ivanov's essay 'Michael Chekhov and Russian Existentialism' in Laurence Senelick (ed.), *Wandering Stars: Russian Emigré Theatre, 1905–1940* (Iowa City, 1992), 155.

2. See Anatoly Smeliansky's essay 'In Search of El Dorado: America in the Fate of the Moscow Art Theatre', in Senelick (ed.), *Wandering Stars*, 44–68.

3. Cited from an interview with Alexander Ostuzhev in Roman Samarin and Alexander Nikolyukin (eds.), *Shakespeare in the Soviet Union* (Moscow, 1966), 158 and 163–4.

4. Rowe, *Hamlet: A Window on Russia*, 128–32. Rowe relies on the personal testimony of Juri Jelagin, who was a member of the Vakhtangov Theatre in Moscow; she also draws on his book *Taming of the Arts* (New York, 1951).

5. Mikhail M. Morozov, *Shakespeare on the Soviet Stage* (London, 1947), 34–40.

6. Cf. Rowe, *Hamlet: A Window on Russia*, 133–4.

7. For the information on Shakespeare in Latvia I am indebted to Laura Raidonis Bate's paper 'The Abuse of Greatness: The Appropriation of

Julius Caesar in Latvia during Periods of Political Transition', presented at the World Shakespeare Congress in Los Angeles, 1996.

8. Dennis Kennedy, *Looking at Shakespeare* (Cambridge, 1993), 108 (with three illustrations, 106–8). The following productions of *Julius Caesar* and *As You Like It* in Prague are also discussed by Kennedy, pp. 100–3 (three illustrations).

9. See the Czech edition *Romeo a Julie* (Prague, 1955), 199–200.

10. See Péter Szaffkó, 'In Search of the "Real" Shakespeare: Sándor Hevesi's Role in the Development of Hungarian Theatre Arts', in Holgar Klein and Péter Dávidházi (eds.), *Shakespeare and Hungary* (Lewiston, NY, 1996), 127.

5. SHAKESPEARE BEHIND THE IRON CURTAIN

1. Quotations are from Eleanor Rowe, *Hamlet: A Window on Russia* (New York, 1976), 148–52. Emma P. Szabo's essay 'Shakespeare's *Hamlet* and Pasternak's Poem' is reprinted in Jerzy Limon and Jay L. Halio (eds.), *Shakespeare and his Contemporaries* (Newark, Del., 1993), 169–74.

2. For the exchange of letters between Pasternak and Kozintsev see Rowe, 153–4 and Grigori Kozintsev, *Shakespeare: Time and Conscience* (New York, 1966), 214–15 and 221.

3. See Jan Kott, *Shakespeare our Contemporary* (3rd edn. New York, 1966), 62; Marta Gibińska, 'Polish Hamlets: Shakespeare's *Hamlet* in Polish Theatres after 1945', in M. Hattaway, B. Sokolova, and D. Roper (eds.), *Shakespeare in the New Europe* (Sheffield, 1994), 159–73.

4. Frank Kermode, *New York Review of Books*, 24 Sept. 1964; out of the many other reviews, a good example of a less severe but penetrating criticism is E. A. J. Honigmann's 'Bouts with the Bard', *Glasgow Herald*, 8 May 1965.

5. See Kott, *Shakespeare our Contemporary*, 48; the following quotations are also from the 3rd New York edn. Some of Kott's glaring mistakes in the 1st edn. were later removed and new essays were added.

6. Mladen Engelsfeld, '*The Tempest* along the Croatian Coast in 1980 and 1981', *Shakespeare Quarterly*, 33 (winter 1982), 505–6.

7. John Elson (ed.), *Is Shakespeare Still our Contemporary?*, proceedings of an international conference (London, 1989), 14–15.

8. An enlarged English version of Kozintsev's book appeared under the title *Shakespeare: Time and Conscience* (New York, 1966; London, 1967). All my quotations are from the 1st edn.

9. Cf. Peter Holland, 'Two-Dimensional Shakespeare: "King Lear" on Film', in Anthony Davies and Stanley Wells (eds.), *Shakespeare and the Moving Image* (Cambridge, 1994), 63.

10. Grigori Kozintsev, *King Lear: The Space of Tragedy* (Berkeley and Los Angeles, 1977), 63. Other direct or indirect quotations from this book are taken from pp. 25, 34, 37, 72, 119, 251.

11. Grigori Kozintsev, 'Hamlet and *King Lear*: Stage and Film', in Clifford Leech and J. M. R. Margeson (eds.), *Shakespeare 1971*, Proceedings of the World Shakespeare Congress, Vancouver, August 1971 (Toronto, 1972), 197.

12. Kenneth S. Rothwell, 'Representing *King Lear* on Screen: From Metatheatre to "Meta-Cinema"', in Davies and Wells (eds.), *Shakespeare and the Moving Image*, 224.

13. Cf. Alexander Lipkov, 'The Artist and Conscience', in A. Anikst (ed.), *Shakespeare Readings 1977* (Moscow, 1980), 290–314 (in Russian).

14. For a chapter on Josef Svoboda see Dennis Kennedy, *Looking at Shakespeare* (Cambridge, 1993), 220–6 (four illustrations).

15. See the programme note of the Theatre on the Balustrade, first night, 31 Jan. 1969; cf. Daniel Gerould's review of the production in Samuel L. Leiter (chief ed.), *Shakespeare around the Globe* (New York, 1986), 726–7.

16. Václav Havel, *Lidové noviny* (People's Newspaper), Prague, 27 July 1990, p. 4.

17. My chief source for discussing Sturua's production of *Richard III* was Alexei Bartoshevich's paper at the World Shakespeare Congress at Stratford-upon-Avon in 1981.

18. Cited from Inga-Stina Ewbank's essay 'Shakespeare Translation as Cultural Exchange', *Shakespeare Survey 48* (1995), 9–10.

19. Cf. Margot Heinemann, 'How Brecht Read Shakespeare', in Jonathan Dollimore and Alan Sinfield (eds.), *Political Shakespeare: New Essays in Cultural Materialism* (Ithaca, NY, 1985), 202–30.

20. See Martin Hilský, 'Shakespeare in Czech: An Essay in Cultural Semantics', in Hattaway et al. (eds.), *Shakespeare in the New Europe*, 150–8. Hilský provided a new Czech translation for the 1987 production which was directed by Karel Kříž.

21. See Joan Montgomery Byles, 'Political Theatre: *Hamlet* in Romania', *Shakespeare Bulletin*, 9 (spring 1991), 25–6; Mark L. Ratner, 'Afi Sau Nu Afi', *Acacia* (Cal State University at Hayward, winter 1987), 4–5.

6. POST-COMMUNIST SHAKESPEARE

1. The Romany *Romeo and Juliet* was reviewed in German by Claus Clemens in *Shakespeare Jahrbuch*, 132 (Bochum, 1996) and in Czech by Jana Červenková in *Literární noviny* (Prague, 1 June 1995).

2. See Janja Ciglar-Žanić's essay 'Recruiting the Bard: Onstage and Offstage Glimpses of Recent Shakespeare Productions in Croatia', in M. Hattaway,

B. Sokolova, and D. Roper (eds.), *Shakespeare in the New Europe* (Sheffield, 1994), 261–75.

3. See R. A. Foakes, *Hamlet versus Lear* (Cambridge, 1993).

4. See Peter Holland, 'Mind the Gap', *Shakespeare Jahrbuch*, 131 (Bochum, 1995) and Alexei Bartoshevich's seminar presentation at the Twenty-Sixth International Shakespeare Conference at Stratford-upon-Avon in 1994 (in typescript).

A Select Bibliography

BATE, JONATHAN, and JACKSON, RUSSELL (eds.), *Shakespeare: An Illustrated Stage History.* Oxford: Oxford University Press, 1996.

BENTLEY, G. E., *The Jacobean and Caroline Stage.* 7 vols. Oxford: Clarendon Press, 1941–68.

BOLDIZSÁR, IVÁN (ed.), *New Hungarian Quarterly*, Shakespeare Memorial Number, 5/13. Budapest: Kossuth Printing House, spring 1964.

COHN, ALBERT, *Shakespeare in Germany in the Sixteenth and Seventeenth Centuries.* London: Asher and Co., 1865; repr. Wiesbaden, 1967.

COHN, RUBY, *Modern Shakespeare Offshoots.* Princeton: Princeton University Press, 1976.

DAVIES, ANTHONY, and WELLS, STANLEY (eds.), *Shakespeare and the Moving Image: The Plays in Films and Television.* Cambridge: Cambridge University Press, 1994.

DELABASTITA, DIRK, and D'HULST, LIEVEN (eds.), *European Shakespeares: Translating Shakespeare in the Romantic Age.* Amsterdam: John Benjamins BV, 1993.

DUŢU, ALEXANDRU, *Shakespeare in Rumania.* Bucharest: Meridiane Publishing House, 1964.

ELSOM, JOHN (ed.), *Is Shakespeare Still our Contemporary?* London: Routledge, 1989.

GIBIŃSKA, MARTA, and LIMON, JERZY (eds.), *Hamlet East–West.* Gdańsk: Theatrum Gedanense Foundation, 1998.

GUNTNER, LAWRENCE, and MCLEAN, ANDREW M. (eds.), *Redefining Shakespeare: Literary Theory and Theater Practice in the German Democratic Republic.* Newark: University of Delaware Press, 1998.

GURR, ANDREW, *The Shakespearian Playing Companies.* Oxford: Clarendon Press, 1996.

HATTAWAY, MICHAEL, SOKOLOVA, BOIKA, and ROPER, DEREK (eds.), *Shakespeare in the New Europe.* Sheffield: Sheffield Academic Press, 1994.

HELSZTYŃSKI, STANISŁAW (ed.), *Poland's Homage to Shakespeare.* Warsaw: Państwowe Wydawnictvo Naukowe, 1965.

HORTMANN, WILHELM, *Shakespeare on the German Stage: The Twentieth Century*, with a section on 'Shakespeare on Stage in the German Democratic Republic' by Maik Hamburger. Cambridge: Cambridge University Press, 1998.

HOTSON, LESLIE, *The Commonwealth and Restoration Stage*. Cambridge, Mass.: Harvard University Press, 1928.

KENNEDY, DENNIS (ed.), *Foreign Shakespeare: Contemporary Performance*. Cambridge: Cambridge University Press, 1993.

—— *Looking at Shakespeare*. Cambridge: Cambridge University Press, 1993.

KLEIN, HOLGAR, and DÁVIDHÁZI, PÉTER (eds.), *Shakespeare and Hungary*, Shakespeare Yearbook, 7. Lewiston, NY: Edwin Mellen Press, 1996.

KOTT, JAN, *Shakespeare our Contemporary*, trans. Boleslaw Taborski. London: Methuen, 1964.

KOZINTSEV, GRIGORI, *Shakespeare: Time and Conscience*, trans. Joyce Vining. New York: Hill & Wang, 1966.

—— *King Lear: The Space of Tragedy*, trans. Mary MacKintosh. Berkeley and Los Angeles: University of California Press, 1977.

LEITER, SAMUEL L. (ed.), *Shakespeare around the Globe: A Guide to Notable Postwar Revivals*. New York: Greenwood Press, 1986.

LEWINTER, OSWALD (ed.), *Shakespeare in Europe: An Anthology of Outstanding Writings on Shakespeare by Europeans*. Cleveland: World Publishing Company, Meridian Books, 1963.

LIMON, JERZY, *Gentlemen of a Company: English Players in Central and Eastern Europe, 1590–1660*. Cambridge: Cambridge University Press, 1985.

—— and HALIO, JAY L. (eds.), *Shakespeare and his Contemporaries*, Eastern and Central European Studies. Newark: University of Delaware Press, 1993.

MOROZOV, MIKHAIL M., *Shakespeare on the Soviet Stage*, trans. David Magarshack. London: Soviet News, 1947.

NUNGEZER, EDWIN, *A Dictionary of Actors and of Other Persons Associated with the Public Representation of Plays in England before 1642*. New Haven, Conn.: Yale University Press, 1929.

PRICE, JOSEPH, and PARFENOV, ALEXANDR (eds.), *Russian Essays*. Newark: University of Delaware Press, 1998.

ROWE, ELEANOR, *Hamlet: A Window on Russia*. New York: New York University Press, 1976.

SAMARIN, ROMAN, and NIKOLYUKIN, ALEXANDER (eds.), *Shakespeare in the Soviet Union*. Moscow: Progress Publishers, 1966.

SCHRICKX, WILLEM, *Foreign Envoys and Travelling Players in the Age of Shakespeare and Jonson*. Wetteren: Universa, 1986.

SENELICK, LAURENCE (ed.), *Wandering Stars: Russian Emigré Theatre, 1905–1940*. Iowa City: University of Iowa Press, 1992.

STŘÍBRNÝ, ZDENĚK (ed.), *Charles University on Shakespeare*. Prague: Universita Karlova, 1966.

WEIMANN, ROBERT, *Shakespeare and the Popular Tradition in the Theatre*, trans. Robert Schwartz. Baltimore: Johns Hopkins University Press, 1978.

WEIMANN, ROBERT, *Authority and Representation in Early Modern Discourse*. Baltimore: Johns Hopkins University Press, 1996.

WELLS, STANLEY, and TAYLOR, GARY (eds.), *William Shakespeare: The Complete Works*. Oxford: Clarendon Press, 1986.

WILLIAMS, SIMON, *Shakespeare on the German Stage*, i: *1586–1914*. Cambridge: Cambridge University Press, 1990.

ZARIAN, ROUBEN, *Shakespeare and the Armenians*. Yerevan: Academy of Sciences Press, 1969.

Index